Celtic Cowhunter

Florida's Cow Culture in Poetry & Prose

To Terry —

Thanks for your friendship. Wishing you all the best!

B 12-9-16

W. Bradley Phares

Cover Design: Andi Norwich
Nth Degree Designs
1318 Lebanon Avenue
Belleville, Illinois

Edited by: Morissa Schwartz

GenZPublishing.org
Aberdeen, NJ

ISBN:

To Sam Phares,
the ballast and beauty in my life,
for her steadfast encouragement in following the dreams of a dreamer.

With special thanks to Jacqueline and Jared Phares and all my family for daily inspiration in making me the person I am, and especially to my Dad and the others who've moved on ahead of us...
Chi mi a-rithist thu.
(I'll see you again)

Contents

Foreword

Growing up in Texas I assumed, like most Texans, that Texas was where cowboys originated, and the cowboy domain ranged from west of Ft. Worth to somewhere in California and included some parts of Mexico and up into western Canada. Every western movie I ever saw from Lonesome Dove to True Grit was in a dusty scene somewhere out West. Later, when I had moved to Tennessee to attempt to become a rich and famous household name, I had yet to see a working ranch, and I thought surely there were no real cowboys on this side of the Mississippi running wild and wooly herds of cattle through the harsh wilds of American frontier, and doing it all horseback, like a dozen generations before him, carrying on the traditions of the American cowboy… nope, those folks were all out West…

Then, I met met Brad Phares.

Since that day some 13 years ago, when the band and I rolled the bus into Okeechobee, Florida to play a show, I have hunted wild hogs and alligators with Brad, caught a ten-pound bass, worked cows, drank beer, smoked briskets, sang songs, drank more beer, rode some good horses, had many great conversations, and have become friends with a family that has almost become like my own family. And I have become educated, as you are about to. Brad has a real passion for history and heritage, and it shows in his writing, his poetry, and his artwork.

Years ago, Brad gave me a hand braided "cracker" whip, which, through much embarrassing trial and painful error, I have since learned to crack without taking my ear off. While gathering cattle one day, I saw Brad use it like it was really meant: he picked out a single cow in a herd and gave it some "inspiration" to move along without touching any of the other cows. I swear he could pick flies off those cows' backs if he wanted. I remember him saying that as a kid he would set a soda can in a tree and practice knocking it off, while other kids were practicing shooting a basketball. Judging from his artwork, he must have spent some time as a kid drawing pictures, too. In fact, he's a hand at just about anything he puts his mind to.

As you read on, what you will soon find out about this award-winning cook (he has his own brand of barbeque sauce!), painter, poet, songwriter, journalist, hunting guide, horse trainer, rancher, and businessman is that his real passion is his family, his heritage, his work, his land, and his livestock. He is a modern cowman that holds dearly to the traditions of the past. His family has run cattle on these grasslands for many, many generations, enduring hurricanes, drought, alligators, politicians, wild cow wrecks, bad broncs, diseases, rustlers, and stock market crashes, just to name a few setbacks, and he and his family are still here and helping to pass it on to another generation.

Not unlike Baxter Black and other cowboy poets, Brad will entertain with each small portrait of ranch life, told in true, old- time cowboy campfire fashion, but with a twist. Brad's book will show you the forgotten story of the "cracker" cowboy, and give you a history lesson on our Scottish and Irish herding ancestors, and you'll possibly gain some insight into why cowboys still like to fight, drink, gamble, and sing sad songs to the fair maidens... Heck, it's in our DNA!

I hope you enjoy this work of art, history, and heritage as much as I have, and I hope you pass it on to someone else who, like us, will appreciate the wisdom, experience, and dedication poured into these tales of humor, love, laughter, tears, hardship, and good ol' cowboy philosophy… and I hope someday you get to meet the humble, talented man who I am proud to call my friend, and shake his hand and see the sincerity in his eyes, and thank him for this rare gift from a real cowboy on the other side of the Mississippi. Happy Trails and Happy Reading!

~Trent Willmon

Prologue

"After nourishment, shelter, and companionship, stories are the thing we need most in the world." ~ Philip Pullman

I've been immersed in stories for as long as I can remember. I remember my mom reading to me and my brothers at night before bedtime on a regular basis, and hearing adults recite family stories to us. I recall writing my own one to two page stories in a spiral notebook, drawing the illustrations to accompany them and getting permission from the teacher, Mrs. Reeves, to stand at the front of the room reading them to my second grade classmates at Lawnwood Elementary. In high school, I found Louis L'Amour books and the cowboy poetry of Baxter Black, Waddie Mitchell and I purchased Cowboy Poetry: The Reunion, which was a compilation of various works published by the Western Folklife Center in Elko, Nevada. I couldn't get enough of any of them and it spurred me to write my first piece of cowboy poetry one summer while driving a tractor disking up ground to plant grass at the ranch. I followed that up by penning a short story in the style of Louis L'Amour during my senior year that went on to deliver me a first place finish in a regional creative writing contest for high school students.

Back then, I thought I'd remember every little detail of every single story that I'd ever been told about ranching in Florida's bygone days along with the name of each person who shared the story. Sadly, too many years had flown by me when I came to learn the harsh reality that the passage of time is unforgiving and robs the mind of what it once held so firmly. Some of the stories vanished from memory completely while others remained, and if not completely intact, then they at least lingered in bits and pieces; broken fragments that leave a person constantly searching through the deepest recesses of the mind hoping to access that which somehow slipped away. Some of them were firsthand accounts while others had been passed down through the family from one generation to the next. They laid out the good times and the bad, and without fail each one captured the imagination carrying you to a distant place and time no matter whether it was your first time hearing a new story or if it was an old favorite that had been recycled a few times.

Agriculturalists, and especially ranchers, tend to be private and humble individuals by and large, so on many levels sharing their personal story or relating how they live is a tough thing for them to do. If they get past the angst of simply having to engage in an extended conversation about their daily routine of ranch life, they're likely to keep it to short, direct answers for fear that they'll come across as being a braggart or too rumbumptious, or perhaps even that they're divulging too much personal information. This is especially true of the older generations. The downside is that it makes for very poor public relations, which is a crucial factor for the agricultural community to consider in these times where the majority of Americans have become too far removed from their rural roots for far too long. Fortunately, there's been a growing recognition amongst farmers and ranchers alike that we have a positive and intriguing story to share with the world; a story which we need to get busy telling as often as possible.

My late recognition of the need to preserve Florida's ranch life (both past and present) with a written record for future generations coupled with my awareness of the disconnect between urban dwellers and those of us providing the food for their tables prompted me to start a blog focused on Florida ranch life. For years, I'd carried the thought in the back of my mind that I wanted to write a few books at some point in time and the secondary function of the blog was to act as a repository for that purpose.

Having explained my compulsion for putting together this collection of stories, poems, and photos, by now there's a couple nagging questions left to be answered for most of you: *what does Celtic have to do with a cowhunter*, and for those new to the term, just *what exactly is a cowhunter anyway*? Quite simply put, it comes down to our cultural heritage and paying homage to it.

In the opening chapter, I'll explain how *Celtic* herding traditions and Scotts-Irish migration patterns to the American Colonies and then within our fledgling nation heavily influenced ranching in Florida, and also the Deep South before spreading across the nation as a whole. The term *Cowhunter* first came into use across Florida during the late 1800's as it was truly indicative of how men who owned or worked cattle located and gathered them...by actually hunting for them scattered throughout the state's rough, wooded range lands, prairies, and boggy marshes over the course of multiple roundups. Another distinguishing feature of cowhunters is their use of cow whips (not to be confused with a bull whip, which is an entirely different instrument) in handling cattle and it is this hallmark which gives rise to the term Florida Cracker as another name used in identifying this group of people. Across the sagebrush covered range of the Great Basin, they're known as Buckaroos, in Hawaii they're called Paniolos, California has the vaquero tradition and in Florida they're Cowhunters. The name varies depending on the region of the country, yet the profession is the same: American Cowboy.

Several excellent books have been previously published laying out the historical facts associated with ranching in Florida and making certain to stress the point that Florida was the first location cattle were landed in the present-day United States. It's a lesser-known fact, and it along with all the other scholarly documentation, are things well-worth being proud of for native Floridians but I wanted to offer all that history in a different way; one that added more layers and texture to what was already known. It's no big secret that most people tied to Florida ranching have always carried a little chip on their shoulder over the fact that for far too many years their role as a foundational pillar in building Florida has been forgotten in their own backyard, and on a larger scale their part in the American ranching story has been overlooked and under-appreciated.

More than an effort to stake Florida's claim as progenitor of American ranching, my aim is to point out the things about Florida's ranching story that make it unique, special and worth preserving. When I set about compiling old stories and writing new ones for this book, I immediately knew that I wanted it to thread together a historical timeline of Florida's cattle culture from past to present that would weave a tapestry highlighting our rich and unique way of life on Florida's ranch lands.

For those who know ranching-the ones who live it out faithfully every single day across our great nation, my hope is that this collection of stories, poems, photographs and illustrations will resurrect some of your own memories and that some of my own which I've offered here might brighten your day. And for my city-dwelling brethren, my aspiration is that the following pages should serve to educate and enlighten you to some little-known but foundational pieces of Florida history that continue to influence the state's culture and traditions today; and, that despite all the concrete and metal of your city landscape, you once again feel a close connection to the natural world along with a deeper appreciation for Florida's beautiful backcountry.

Chapter 1

A Cow Culture and its Characters

Ranching In America: A Southern Birth

Prevailing thought and popular opinion has always held that ranching as we know it had its earliest beginnings in the American West. Quite to the contrary, cattle ranching was birthed in the South by two cultures bearing well-established traditions of herding-The Spanish along with the Scots-Irish and Briton descendants of Celts-a fact that is completely overlooked by the vast majority of Americans and presumably by most anyone around the world. When the question as to where the first cattle appeared in present-day America is posed to nearly anyone, more likely than not, they will mention Texas or California. In so doing, they would be only partially correct in the fact that herdsmen traditions of early Spanish colonies influenced the birth of American ranching. The location as to where those colonies and that influence first occurred is quite to the contrary.

As nearly all native Floridians know, cattle first stepped onto Florida's sandy shores in 1521 during the course of Ponce de León's second voyage to Florida. In the 16th century, the only other cattle on the North American continent or near its vicinity were in other Spanish colonies within northern Mexico, and possibly a few scattered islands in the Caribbean. Though they've garnered little notoriety outside of Florida or the Gulf Coast region, there are several books such as Florida Cowman, by Joe A. Akerman, Jr., along with a myriad of journal articles all attesting to the aforementioned facts.

Professor Akerman notes that while it is difficult to say whether any of these original Andalusian cattle and horses of Spanish barb and Arab ancestry actually survived the wilds of early Florida, there can be no question that as Spain continued to colonize the new territory they knew as La Florida, they certainly continued to bring additional livestock with them as Franciscan friars established early missions and ranchos throughout the panhandle region. As colonization efforts continued and more livestock was transplanted, Spain's cattle raising efforts thrived in the wilds of territorial Florida during the 17th century but oddly enough the Spaniards seemed to overlook the economic significance of cattle. Indeed, historical accounts reflect that stock raising's significance relating to social status seemed paramount to economic concerns for the Spanish.

Colonial Florida was occupied by many cultures and whether the herdsmen were Spanish, Creek/Seminole or Miccosukee, British, French, or early American settlers, cowmen and cattle have been upon her soil for almost 500 years. Even though Spain managed to claim Florida for 200 years–excluding a twenty year period during which the British and French each took turns trying to pry her away in the years 1763 to 1783–it seems as though Spain was either unwilling or unable to fully devote enough time and resources on its flailing colonial venture to take full advantage of cattle ranching; an enterprise that would soon prove to be Florida's first industry. Perhaps, the Spanish government was too weakened and exhausted from expending so much energy on colonial exploits in Mexico and other areas of Latin America?

Others, like the aforementioned native tribes–who actually became the most important herdsmen on the peninsula during the 18th century–and early white settlers who began to trickle into the territory throughout the late 1700's, recognized the importance of cattle for the future. Florida's early days of colonization may have spawned cattle raising in North America, but there's much more to the story of ranching and its southern roots than solely this portion of historical events taking place in the Florida territory.

Celtic Ways in the Carolinas

As Spain slowly began to lose its grip on the Florida colony, simultaneously and further to the north, another group of immigrants steeped in herding traditions were hitting the shores of the Carolinas and bringing their culture with them. Beginning late in the 17th century, Scots-Irish emigrants poured into the colonies primarily through the ports of Philadelphia, Pennsylvania and New Castle, Delaware, where they quickly moved into the surrounding countryside. Some of those North

Britons, like my dad's family who first moved up the Delaware River, eventually migrated westward into the rolling hills of interior Pennsylvania and beyond. However, the vast majority of these emigrants drifted south and west following the Appalachian Mountains down to the southern highlands of the Carolinas, Tennessee, and Georgia. Surname distributions from the first U.S. Census of 1790 bear out this point as fact showing that although immigrants from North Britain and Ireland found their expanded into every part of the American Colonies, their heaviest concentrations were in the southern highlands.

As it turns out, this migration and settlement pattern was not by mere happenstance, but rather it was because the early American environment in the Appalachian belt mirrored with near perfection the geographical and political tendencies of the border regions they had left behind them across the Atlantic. The Scottish lowlands and the Anglo-Scottish border had been a region notorious for violence and transience, most especially so from the thirteenth through to the beginning of the seventeenth centuries as Scotland and England engaged in a seemingly never-ending battle for control over the borders. Families within the region sought to insulate themselves from the instability by forming clans with a rigid system of beliefs and loyalty. For these early settlers moving into the American backcountry, they found it to be a similarly dangerous environment in comparison to the Anglo-Scottish border region. As such, one might say that these borderers were in their element and as such, they were better suited for this lawless and uncontrolled setting than other settlers. More than anywhere else in the American backcountry, the southern highlands were ideally suited to the Celt descendants' overall ethos, family structure, warrior ethic, and their farming and herding economy.

These Scots-Irish immigrants were direct descendants of Celts, which in the most general terms can be described as a warrior/herder society of the more rural and undomesticated parts of the outer British Isles, such as Scotland, Ireland, Wales, Cornwall and the Northwest fringes of England proper such as Cumbria, Lancashire, and Northumberland. Though the ancient Celts were in fact the aboriginal inhabitants of most all of Western Europe, for simplicity's sake, consider them to be the predominant culture which settled into those outlying areas of the British Isles just mentioned. The Celts were herdsmen and their way of life revolved around raising stock and a pastoral economy.

In his thought-provoking and controversial book, Cracker Culture: Celtic Ways in the Old South, Grady McWhiney sets forth his Celtic-herdsman theory essentially claiming that the influence of Celtic descendants on Southern culture far exceeded their numbers as immigrants and furthermore that the influence persists and continues to this day. Carl Bridenbaugh, a historian with specific expertise in Colonial America, seemed to support much of this theory when he wrote in his book, Myths and Realities, "The conquest of the [backcountry] was achieved by families...The fundamental social unit, the family, was preserved intact...in a transplanting and reshuffling of European folkways." Family in this sense referred to the dual nature of the family structure utilized by the Celt descendants: nuclear core within four generations and a larger layer of kinship, the clan.

In short and simple terms, these descendants from the hinterlands of Northwestern Europe imported their love of stock raising to America with them and began laying the foundation in the South for what would spread across the country to become an iconic American institution...cattle ranching. According to Terry G. Jordan, in his book Trails to Texas: Southern Roots of Western Cattle Ranching, the Carolinas were the "hearth" of open range cattle raising in 17th century America and that the practice went on to spread from there with the onset of the Westward Expansion movement.

Families that have been in the cattle business for a long time have often said ranching must simply be something in your blood and they talk about how it's difficult to explain any other way. For many ranch families today, cattle don't supply the main source of income for the individuals or the ranch itself and these families are raising cattle because it's what they know, it's what they love, and they feel bound to it like it's in their blood. For them, ranching is a matter of family legacy and pride. Based on Mr.

McWhiney's theory, history and genetics seem to suggest there's quite a bit more to the often relayed sentiment that, "ranching is in the blood" than it merely being a trite saying… It may quite possibly be a matter of fact.

All of these historical considerations point to the fact that two different groups of people with ancient herding roots, the Spanish and the Scots-Irish, each combined to lay foundational cornerstones for the rise of American cattle ranching in the colonies of Florida and the Carolinas, respectively. Scots-Irish immigrants defined not only American ranching but the South as a whole, both during that early period and as we know both entities today.

The Celtic-Herdsman Theory and Its Impact on Cattle in the South

As previously mentioned, this Celtic-herdsman theory proposed by Grady McWhiney, a retired Texas Christian University professor, states that the character traits of Scots-Irishmen are a direct result of their ancestral lineage to the Celts, that they imported these traits and customs with them and furthermore, that the sheer numbers of these immigrants dominated the Southern landscape in such a way so as to leave a permanent cultural imprint that persists to the present day. First and foremost, the ancient Celts were warrior/herdsmen. Celtic tribes dominated the British Isles having a pastoral economy and without question their culture revolved around raising stock–whether cattle, sheep or horses. As global civilization evolved, the direct descendants of these tribes remained in the outlying, wild and harsh areas of the British Isles such as Scotland, Ireland, Wales and the northwestern side of England near the Scottish borderlands. Based on where and how they lived, Celts were naturally hardy, fiercely independent, highly adaptive, and ferocious protectors of family and property. All of these characteristics were predicated on a deeply rooted code of honor.

A review of ancient civilizations will reveal that many of history's fiercest and most resilient warrior societies had agrarian herding economies. Warrior/herder societies such as the Hittites, the ancient

Hebrews, and of course the Celts, all shared the themes of self-sufficiency and trading in livestock. Many historical researchers argue that herding societies tend to produce cultures of honor that encourage and emphasize courage, strength, and violence due to the fact that as compared to other forms of agriculture like farming, animal herds are more vulnerable to theft thereby necessitating martial valor and strength. Moreover, possessing these qualities alone was not enough, as the tribal member, clansman, or family member must also be willing to use them for the protection of the herds. The safety of the stock was crucial to their survival and livelihood and required defending at all cost. Developing a reputation for martial skill was equally important because it created a deterrent effect for would-be thieves. Considering that little changed environmentally in the outlying areas of the British Isles for hundreds of years, these core values transcended generations and became a steadfast component of the culture there. And quite likely, a strong case could be made that aside from phenotypic variations or environmental influences, genetic factors common amongst the Celtic people played a key role in propagating a stoic and tenacious populace typical of herding societies.

Celtic Herding Influences in the South

When these Scots-Irishmen and their families crossed the Atlantic and poured into seaports along the coastlines of the colonies from the late 1700's through the antebellum period, their gritty determination and warrior-bred honor code hit southern soil with them. The 1790 Census showed that in fact, 90% of the backcountry settlers in the southern highlands were either Irish, Scottish, or English hailing principally from Ulster, the Scottish lowlands or border region, and from just across the border in the north of England. Further historical records indicate that by 1860, 50% of the southern population was comprised of Scots-Irish peoples. In addition, these rough and tumble immigrants also brought along their penchant for herding as well as importing their love of whiskey, music and poetry, leisure, gambling, and hunting. More importantly, these herdsmen held an aggressive stance towards the world and a pronounced wariness towards outsiders for fear they might try to steal or take livestock and other property. In fact, there are references in personal letters and writings from 1717 where the Quakers of Pennsylvania noted that the influx of North Britons had also imported with themselves the ancient border habit of bullheadedness and disdain towards other ethnic groups. Instead, they embraced and encouraged a sense of stubborn autonomy amongst their families and clan groups. Fully committed and engaged in all things, the Scots-Irish played as hard as they worked thereby placing a premium on having spare time at their disposal for leisure activities; open range herding allowed them to do exactly that. They turned their stock loose on common pasture or in the woods and went back to collect them when needed.

Depiction of Irish cattle raid in 1581

In Cracker: Celtic Ways in the Old South, professor McWhiney points out that aside from the shared cultural and psychological traits, the Scots-Irish settlers incorporated many herding characteristics originating in their native homelands of Scotland, Ireland, Wales and Northwest England. These practices included the following just to name a few: marking and branding of stock; collection at regular intervals of herds at established penning areas; a heavy reliance on shepherd dogs in cowhunts and herd management; use of whips; overland cattle drives to feeder areas/markets along regularly used trails performed by professional or semi-professional drovers; seasonal movement of stock; use of open range; accumulation of very large herds numbering from the hundreds to the thousands; use of hired, indentured or enslaved cow hands to compile a workforce beyond the immediate family; and range burning to improve forage sources.

Bolstering Mr. McWhiney's assertions is the 1773 account given by a surveyor for the colony of South Carolina in which he noted a grazing system whereby expansive herds of cattle, many times numbering over a thousand animals, were raised in the woods in the backcountry region between the Savannah and Ogechee Rivers. He went on to elaborate as to how they were tended by "gangs under the auspices of cow-pen keepers, which move from forest to forest in a measure as the grass wears out or the planters approach them." Finally, the animals were rounded up, penned, and driven to market on the hoof.

Documented interviews with natives of Scotland describe the Highlanders as being "averse to enclosures" and points out their opposition to fenced pastures due to the view of it as "a much more expensive way of grazing their cattle than letting them run as they do in the hills." Accounts shared from Ireland natives relate that the "neighbors have a lingering habit of ignoring the fences." Cattle grazing in the southern colonies was conducted in the same fashion whereby the stock freely roamed the woods and any common pasturelands gathered into pens only when there was a need to sell a few. Early in the 18th century, visitors to South Carolina commented on seeing smaller sized black animals that appeared to be of British origin prevalent throughout the colonial southeast. Englishmen who came as visitors to the southern colonies reported seeing "small black cattle, not unlike Irish cattle" while others described "black cattle small of size, but strong".

An art print of a Yemassee raid on the South Carolina frontier during the Yemassee War of 1715. Library of Congress collection

Around this same time period, British governor of South Carolina, James Moore, decided to mount an invasion of Florida against the Spanish and in doing so, he set the stage for the first white settlers, Scots-Irishmen and their families, to begin trickling into Georgia and northern Florida. Some of them moved herds with them on their journey, while others simply moved their families and slowly built herds by collecting stock left behind by the Spaniards. Unlike the Spanish, these families with their long history of herding realized the opportunity to prosper at raising cattle and seized upon it. Whether they brought their herds with them or acquired them as they moved, these herdsmen-settlers were all drawn to territorial Florida for one major reason: its rich rangelands and the wild cattle grazing upon them.

The stage was set for these Scots-Irish families to follow in the footsteps of their Celtic ancestors as they moved into the outlying fringes both south and west of the original colonial borders expanding cattle production and perfecting their legacy as herdsmen. Throughout the remainder of the 18th century, these hardy, adaptive families and their livestock continued streaming into the backcountry of North Carolina, South Carolina, Georgia and north Florida. As the Westward Expansion movement gained traction in the 1800's, the Scots-Irish led the way. And down to the south, as Spain continued to lose control of Florida ultimately signing it over to the U.S. under a treaty in 1819, yet again the movement was led by Scots-Irishmen. Their small and sturdy black cattle crossbred with the Spanish scrub cattle forming the seedstock for Florida cattle herds today, and as professor Jordan documents so well in Trails to Texas: Southern Roots of Western Cattle Ranching, Scotts-Irishmen also made the long and winding trek to the Mississippi River, Texas and beyond.

Early Florida cattle in Punta Rassa awaiting shipment to Cuba. Photo courtesy Florida State Archives, My Florida Memory Project

Another photo from the Florida Archives showing early cattle on the beach in NW Florida. Photo courtesy Florida State Archives

Celtic Influence Beyond Herding

An oft-quoted line by an unknown source claims "you can't tell where you are going unless you know where you've been." Indeed, those few simple words enshrine volumes of truth and it's especially pertinent in the context of American ranching origins as well as the whole of America's birth. Examining where we've been requires an additional look at the settlement patterns of the early American Colonies. Back in the British Isles, the Celts were very much anti-English, a sentiment that echoes even today. These deep-rooted sentiments crossed the Atlantic to the American Colonies as each group carried its culture with it and the same animosities that existed in the old country continued in the new.

While Celt descendants from Ireland, Scotland and borderland regions of Britain settled predominantly into the southern colonies, the northern U.S. was largely settled by farmers from the more domesticated and urbane south and east sides of England as well as more established countries like the Netherlands and Germany. The English and other northern settlers were crop growers; more worldly, strict, White Anglo-Saxon Protestants who followed the Protestant work ethic, and ascribed to an entirely different system of honor. Progressing through the years, the North began to equate honor with economic success and moral character due to its industrialized economy while the South still thrived on an agrarian economy rooted in the herding honor code described earlier.

Essentially, Mr. McWhiney asserts that the War Between the States was an inevitable conclusion based solely on the settlement patterns and cultural differences that had long been festering. Although most critics focus on his idea as being without merit for being overly simplified, there are scores of documents, books and other historical evidence articulating the fact that more than anything else, the Civil War was predicated on conflicting ideals and needs of the agrarian economy of the South versus the industrial-based economy of the North and how they related to principles of states' rights. How can one deny that the respective cultures of each geographical area form the basis for those economies? One could potentially argue that these divergent notions of honor, culture and lifestyle not only precipitated the Civil War, but continue to shape the dynamics of American society and politics today—urban versus rural, liberal versus conservative, and so forth.

Mr. McWhiney's assertions and conclusions on the Celtic-herdsman influence in general have been widely criticized by other scholars and researchers as overly broad and simplistic. Their most significant rebuttal to his theory is that cultures do not remain unaltered or static over the generations, but rather they evolve with technological advances, changes in environmental conditions and so forth. While this may in fact be true, the similarities between Celtic culture and antebellum southern culture seems entirely too strong to sweep away dismissively. To better illustrate the point, recall the accounts referenced earlier relating the native Celt's disdain for fencing and then consider the fact that Florida, who was inundated with Scots-Irish settlers, did not enact a fence law until 1949. Such a parallel is no small coincidence.

As further evidence of the Celtic influence in the Deep South, consider also the fact that the Confederate Battle Flag design was in fact inspired by the St. Andrew's Cross, The Saltire, which is the principal component of Scotland's national flag (the oldest in Europe). In similar fashion, Florida's state flag features a red St. Andrew's cross on white background, perhaps influenced by both the predominant Scots and Irish lineage of its citizenry given that a red diagonal cross on white background serves as another symbol for Ireland and St. Patrick (who in point of fact, was a Scot himself).

The South may not have been an exact replica of Celtic culture in the British Isles, but the stark and striking similarities between the core values and cultural ideals cannot be denied. They are an underlying foundation that is pervasive, persistent and clearly perpetuated.

Two independent and distinct herding cultures–Spanish and Celtic–had each begun propagating cattle in a new world, but it was the strong, persistent and aggressive characteristics of the Scotts-Irish that would lead them to capture the livestock remnants of diminished Spanish glory and cast it into Florida's oldest industry. Simultaneously, other immigrants with the same Celtic heritage moved west instead of south carrying livestock with them on their journey. And oddly enough, Spanish Andalusian and Corriente cattle would once again become a key component of American ranching as they drifted north into Texas and the southwestern U.S. from Mexico to greet those settlers. Prevailing thought for most people has always been that ranching started in the American southwest, but a deeper historical record reveals that American cattle herds and ranching found their origins in the Deep South.

"Land, until it is highly civilized and urbanized, gets the kind of people who are suited to it..."

~ George MacDonald Fraser, author
"The Steel Bonnets: The story of the Anglo-Scottish Border Reivers"

If we forget or destroy our roots, we cannot grow in the future.

~ Gaelic Proverb

Nine Generations Strong: A Family's Ranching Legacy

For a great many reasons, our family keeps a large number of old family photos, awards and honors, along with other memorabilia prominently displayed in our homes. The biggest reasons for doing so would be pride in our family legacy, pride in both the personal work and public service accomplishments done by our forefathers and the unwavering knowledge that our future is forged by our past.

I count my blessings every day that I was born into an agrarian family that is deeply rooted, on both my paternal and maternal sides, in a tradition of working upon and preserving the land. In comparison to my mom's paternal family lineage, the Pearce family, much less research and family records exist relative to my dad's family, although I have established thus far that they consist of an extensive line of mercenary warriors, blacksmiths,and farmers hailing from Scotland and Ireland.

As mentioned previously, early Scotts-Irish immigrants settled the colonial south and over the course of many years introduced and dispersed the culture's herding traditions across the United States. Not all colonial migration was westward out of The Thirteen Colonies; some of those early settlers migrated from the Carolinas south into Georgia then eventually found their way to Florida. Award winning author Patrick Smith chronicles that historical migration by use of a fictional family in his classic book "A Land Remembered", and the Pearces are just one of many families who are a living testament of its occurrence.

John Pearce has been an overwhelmingly popular name in my family, as numerous variations of them existed in each generation. However, the first documented John Pearce was a

Revolutionary War veteran who initially owned land in Bladen County, North Carolina. As the state of Georgia was being settled by conferring land grants to enterprising pioneers, John Pearce moved to Washington County, Georgia sometime in 1800. The family's herding traditions and migration continued when, in October of 1827, John wrote a will stipulating his wish that his heirs were to sell the land he had drawn in a land lottery and utilize the proceeds to procure stock cattle and move into the Florida territory. Shortly after executing the will, John passed away and by 1830, census documents indicate that his widow, Ann Cain Pearce, was residing in Lulu, Columbia County, Florida near the town of Alligator, later to become known as Lake City, Florida.

Levi Pearce, who was born in 1806 as the sixth child out of ten, had moved to Florida with the family and their livestock where he and his wife, Mary Jane Hooker saw the birth of their eldest son, John Mizell Pearce on November 17, 1834. John Mizell was so named for his Pearce grandfather and for the Mizell family into which several Pearce relatives had married. Levi served in various military companies during the Indian Wars of colonial America and in Florida established a reputation as an outstanding Methodist circuit rider. Based on his military record, Reverend Levi Pearce applied for land under the Armed Occupation Act resulting in the family moving south once more to the Alafia River area of Hillsborough County, Florida, much further south and west of Columbia County where the family and their herds would continue to grow.

John Mizell Pearce grew up to serve in numerous volunteer companies-with Captain William Hooker's Company being among them-during the Third Seminole War which spanned the years 1855-1858. Some of his duties involved scouting and surveying Seminole activities in the Kissimmee Valley area and he first witnessed the beautiful area that would later become the Pearce Homestead near Fort Basinger while engaged in one such scouting expedition.

In early 1858, John Mizell Pearce married Martha Ann Lanier in Manatee County establishing themselves along the Peace River near Fort Meade where he had already become a prominent cattleman with extensive holdings and in fact, by 1862, records indicate that he had 830 head of cows.

As these conflicts settled down, yet another loomed just ahead with the nation inching ever closer to the onset of the Civil War. Florida, with its burgeoning beef industry and cattle inventories estimated at just under 700,000 head in 1862 would prove to be pivotal for the Confederacy. In fact, with Texas and other western states cut off by Union forces, Florida became the last viable source of beef for the Confederacy in 1863. A robust cattle trade with Cuba had begun in the 1850's and soon became disrupted by a Union naval blockade in the early days of the war. Excluding Key West and Tampa, only about 3,500 of the state's 140,000 residents lived south of Kissimmee and with cattle outnumbering people in Florida by a ratio of five to one, Florida held more than an ample supply of beef for the Confederacy. The only thing remotely close to a disadvantage was the fact that the bulk of the cattle grazed ranges in the lower part of the peninsula such that it took 30-45 days to drive them out of South Florida 300-400 miles to railheads in Georgia from where they could be distributed throughout the southern states. Hampered by Union raiding parties and even Confederate deserters, the supply of cattle driven north proved to be inconsistent and a lingering problem until 1864 when the First Battalion, Florida Special Cavalry, better known to many as the Cow Cavalry, Cattle Guard Battalion or the Home Guard was mustered under the command of Major Charles J. Munnerlyn. The battalion consisted of nine companies totaling 800 men patrolling from Fort Myers to Georgia with the special reserve group's specific duties being that of renewing free and efficient movement along the cattle drives and also defending against cattle forays perpetrated by Union troops.

For his part, John Mizell Pearce enlisted with Captain F. A. Hendry's Company of the Cow Cavalry sometime in 1863 where he served as a 1st Sergeant until the surrender in 1865. Captain F. A. Hendry's Company of 131 men, was posted at Fort Meade and were deemed so effective in thwarting Union cattle rustlers that any cattle thefts in the area from Fort Meade south to Fort Myers were nearly brought to a standstill. In fact, Major Munnerlyn's first official report indicated that this unit was the most proficient within the battalion resulting in all Cattle Guard companies except for a couple in the panhandle region to be consolidated under Hendry's command. Despite being an irregular unit, the troops within the Cow Cavalry possessed all the requisite loyalty, skills and knowledge causing them to be especially fitted to their duties of providing protection to the settlers of Central and South Florida and procuring and delivering much needed supplies. The theater of operations in which they served was terrain that they knew better than anyone else. Though short-lived against the backdrop of the entire War Between the States, the Cow Cavalry was undeniably vital to the Confederacy by ensuring the continued supply of beef all the way through to the formal surrender of Confederate forces at Tallahassee, Florida in May 1865.

The developing Cuban market for Florida cattle which had blossomed in the prior decade was still waiting at the conclusion of the war so upon conclusion of their duties, life for men like John Mizell Pearce changed very little as they continued herding cattle much like they had always done; the only difference being that the buyer and the direction of the cattle drives had changed as Florida cowmen once again returned their focus to the Gulf coast shipping ports.

In exploring Celtic herding influences that were ushered into America with early settlers and likewise the character traits associated with them, the Celts and their descendants seemed to prefer the unsettled, outland areas for habitation and had a distinct aversion to fences or confinement. The trait seems to be a dominant one that is very well ingrained because according to family stories told by my great grandfather, John Olan Pearce, Sr., in an interview with the Miami Herald's Al Burt, John Mizell Pearce fled Polk County and Fort Meade in 1875 because "it was getting too crowded and he was looking for better grass." To highlight the humor of this "overcrowding" observation, one only need consider that Fort Meade's population in 2013 consisted of only 5,802 people, so perhaps the thoughts of all that lush grazing land John Mizell had spotted along the Kissimmee River in his earlier years was the primary motivation in moving the family further south.

Nonetheless, John Mizell Pearce settled with his family on the western side of the Kissimmee River near old Fort Basinger where he continued to build the family cattle business on the surrounding open prairies, served for many years in the capacity of deputy sheriff being the only law enforcement officer in the lower Kissimmee Valley, while also operating a ferry operation across the river charging rates as follows: Man and horse, 25 cents; horse and buggy, 50 cents; a yoke of oxen and cart, 40 cents. Although the details are sparse, it seems as though there was only one steamboat in operation on the Kissimmee River in the 1880's and it was the 47 foot Mary Belle. She was originally owned by Kissimmee's first storekeeper, Major J. H. Allen and her last owner prior to her demise was Captain John Mizell Pearce. In addition to ferrying people and supplies across the river, Captain Pearce also navigated up and down the Kissimmee on the Mary Belle as steamboats were the most efficient and cheapest way to ship goods throughout the interior of Florida's frontier where there were no railways present.

Clearly, the Pearces hadn't evaded crowding and neighbors for too long it seems because in establishing the steamboat service with the town of Kissimmee, the settlement of Basinger began to grow across the river and away from the old fort and the Pearce Homestead. Other cattlemen soon sought out the rich prairies in the area and Basinger's population grew to nearly 500 residents, quite sizable for a South Florida frontier town without a chamber of commerce or any other civic clubs in that period of time. Like most other cowtowns of the day, Basinger had wide streets and boardwalks where it was not uncommon for cattle to oftentimes meander through the main part of town which consisted of five general mercantile stores, three blacksmith shops, a saddle, harness, and shoe shop, two churches, a school, a post office and of course the boat landing.

An example of early Florida scrub cows in some cow pens.

The Pearce Homestead consisted of several homes in Basinger. This home (above) belonged to Martha Lanier Pearce (far right). Photo credit: www.lamartin.com

Other Pearce homes in Basinger

Photo of the Mary Belle from a copy of a Sun Sentinel article.

However, John Mizell Pearce's time as a boat captain was not meant to last as misfortune found his steamboat. In "Okeechobee Boats and Skippers" by Lawrence E. Will, the incidents surrounding the Mary Belle's untimely end can be summed up as follows: Having been north towards Kissimmee, Captain John Mizell Pearce had only a novice crew on board with him as he headed back down river to Basinger. A stop was required at Grape Hammock, just south of Kenansville, to deliver some goods to a fellow by the name of Bill Willingham who was notorious for being a bad seed. Supposedly, "everyone was a-scared of him on account of his killin's and his cuttin' up…" To the surprise of none on board, they made landing and found Willingham in his usual condition – drunk and belligerent. He pulled his knife on Captain Pearce, but he and his boys outmanned Willingham and tied him up. Pearce directed the skeleton crew of inexperienced men to take the boat back down to

Basinger while he made use of an oxcart to haul Willingham to the Sheriff back north in Orlando. Evidently, these men got the idea stuck in their minds that if they did make it to Basinger as instructed, then upon their next trip up river, Willingham would be waiting for them with a gun. Rational thinking was tossed aside as they concocted a scheme to make the impending events look accidental and intentionally sank the Mary Belle near Fort Basinger.

Perhaps this was for the best, a component of God's greater plan to further the family's cattle business. In the 1870-1880 era, Florida cattle herds could range from 5,000 to 50,000 head. Captain Pearce continued amassing cattle and drove herds through the Florida woods, across the expansive prairies and swam them across the Caloosahatchie River to the stockyards at the Gulf Coast port of Punta Rassa [present-day North Fort Myers] where they were loaded onto boats destined for Cuba. John Mizell Pearce would then make the return trip home to Fort Basinger where he would greet his family with saddle bags filled with Spanish gold. The family cattle business continued to thrive as the family grew and according to my great grandmother Gertrude Pearce or "Nana" as we all called her, during a 1989 interview with The Okeechobee News, "Grandfather Pearce was a smart man in many ways. Grandfather Pearce gave every one of his children a certain 10 acres of land where they could put an orange grove or whatever on it. When his children began to come along, he assigned each one of them a family brand. Dock Pearce, the firstborn, was P-1. Aunt Laurel was P-2. It went right on down through the children.

Dock Pearce, my great-great grandfather married Mary V. Roberts at Basinger in the summer of 1884 and went on to become the parents of five children: Lena, Lamar, Gordon, John Olan and Sallie Charlotte. Like his father before him, Dock Pearce gave his children their start in the cattle business. Born in 1895, John Olan Pearce was my great grandfather and at the age of 15 he had his own brand bestowed upon him by his father. His herd would carry his initials, the OP brand.

Dock and Mary Pearce

During the later years of his life, when we great grandkids came into the picture he was "Big Daddy" to all of us. He lived up to that name in every way based on his features and the stories he carried from his life experiences. For now, suffice to say that he grew up on the Pearce homestead west of Basinger in a frame house nestled atop a live oak covered bluff about a half-mile from the Kissimmee River. With the Mary Belle long since gone, a new flat-bottomed stern-wheeler steamboat out of Kissimmee and owned by Captain Clay Johnson would deliver mail and supplies along the Kissimmee River Valley. In his 1975 interview with Al Burt [which by the way is reprinted in his book, "The Tropic of Cracker"] Big Daddy indicated that, "If you wanted a shirt, that's how you got it. If a letter came, it would have to come on that boat." The steamboat would also pick up boxes of citrus grown by the surrounding families and haul them to market in Kissimmee, which was linked to the world by railway.

In 1910 when Big Daddy made his first visit, Okeechobee was just getting its start as a little town called "Tantie" with the only structures of significance to be found being the old schoolhouse and L.M. Raulerson's store within a log building. Big Daddy moved to Okeechobee in 1925 as a married man looking for work to supplement his beginning cattle business. Big Daddy and Nana had three children: John Olan "J.O." Pearce, Jr., who was my granddaddy, Forrest "Hunky" Pearce, and Geraldine Pearce who perished in an accident as an infant. Much like his father, Granddaddy took on other work to supplement his growing cattle business and while working with a road construction company in North Carolina, he met my Granny, Marian Dillard Pearce. Back in Okeechobee, they would raise three children: Nancy Ann Pearce, my mom, John Olan "Joe" Pearce III, and Keith Gordon Pearce.

(L-R) Jim Daughtry, True Story Sr, John Olan Pearce Sr.(Big Daddy), Eddie Sapp and two unidentified men standing behind the gate pause from their work in the cow pens.

By this time, the days of open range ranching were drawing to a close. Gone were the days out on the Kissimmee Prairie were multiple families' cattle commingled and grazed together, but true to their ways of vigilantly searching for the best grazing, my family stuck with the prairies on the west banks of the Kissimmee River as they moved southward to the west shoreline of Lake Okeechobee where they began to purchase ranch land. At first, the family operated together as a whole from where the mouth of the Kissimmee River enters Lake Okeechobee down to near Lakeport. Over the course of time, the family grew, generations came and went, and the ranch was divided between the various family branches. While all of that prairie may not be under common ownership anymore, much of it is still preserved by the same family where we still live and ranch to this day. Granddaddy gave each of us grandkids our own brands as youngsters and through the years, gave us calves and heifers to begin our own herds.

After more than 185 years have passed, the ninth generation of the Pearce family's American cattle tradition is alive and well in my kids, my nieces and nephew, and the children of our cousins, second cousins and so on as they grow up ranching alongside us. And like all of the fathers who preceded me, I gave each of my kids their own brands soon after they were born. As they grew older, they were given their own heifers with which to build their own herds. With a little bit of love and luck, the not-too-distant future will find 10th generation American (9th generation Florida) cattlemen continuing the family tradition.

Pearce cattle near Basinger in the late 1800's/early 1900's.

Banks of the Caloosahatchie

On the Caloosahatchee River
Where it meets the Gulf of Mexico,
He sits shaded on the southern bank
Remembering days of long ago.
His ancestors and others like them
Brought steers here to be sold…
Florida beef for island neighbors
Paid for with coins of Spanish gold.

He sees old ghosts on tall ships
hoisting shadowy sails straight up,
And he toasts them with aged bourbon
Poured in a simple Dixie cup...
They're loaded with his family's cattle
Charting a course for the Florida Straits;
From Punta Rassa to Havana...
Florida beef to Cuban plates.

The facts are all recorded
Detailing all the lore and history;
And his family passed on tales
Of their enduring cattle legacy.
They fondly recalled the days
When cows outnumbered people
And the saddle was your pew,
On a prairie church with no steeple.

In Florida's swamps and on her plains,
They worked hard and carved a life
Raising up kids and herds of cattle
In spite of all the frontier strife.

Whether times were thin or flush
With no luxuries, cars or trains
They endured wet, freezing winters
And flooding waters from hurricanes.

Pioneer families built their fortunes
and forged eternal legacies
Driving wild and wooly cattle
From inland prairie to ports at sea.
Cuban trade built an industry
And in turn helped create a state.
Because there ain't no disputing it,
Beef's what made Florida great.

On the Caloosahatchee River
Where it meets the Gulf of Mexico,
He sits shaded on the southern bank
Remembering days of long ago.
His ancestors and others like them
Brought steers here to be sold…
Florida beef for island neighbors
Paid for with coins made of Spanish gold.

Graveside Morning

Just a hint of smoke drifts through the cedars, oaks and pines
And west through the woods, traffic on a crowded highway whines.
Ain't much breeze stirring so it's mostly quiet and still...
Leaves are droppin' but we've yet to feel autumn's first chill.
This early in the day the shadows stretch heavy, deep and blue
As I pause at the cemetery while daylight's breaking new.

In the golden light of an early October morn,
All the headstones shine, even those that are aged and worn.
Quietly, I sit amongst them at the foot of family graves.
Having ridden by to contemplate on all that they gave...
What they left us, what we've made of it, what remains to do...
Have we followed their example steadfast, faithful and true?

Can't find the reason for feeling so solitary and alone,
But damn I sure feel restless and uneasy down in my bones.
I'm content in the present yet yearn for some of the past...
Like youthful moments with kin that now seem fleeting and fast.
My thoughts are interrupted by the familiar sounds of a crow,
Cut short itself as a haunting, distant train horn blows.

Nearby calves bawl for mama cows; I relish in their sounds.
A perfect serenade for the cowmen buried here in this ground.
You can't see where you're going without knowing where you've been...
Guess that's partly why I'm compelled to come by here now and then.
The sun's climbing higher now and work goes on for the living,
So I best be on my way this early October morning.

Pearce family cemetery at the Pearce Homestead, Basinger, FL

Chapter 2

Rooted in Firm Beliefs & Family

Those Old Cowpens

Silhouetted all alone
or maybe shrouded by some trees
Like the Royal Guard at Buckingham,
they stand stalwart as you please.
Just some poles and lumber
to passersby on the busy highway
With a rough and worn appearance
of weather-beaten brown and gray,
Their history's shaped by work they've seen,
plus sunlight, rain and winds.
Yes sir, there's more than meets the eye
within those old cowpens.

They've seen it all, my friend,
from soggy summers when hurricanes blew
To hard packed ground and clouds of dust
when droughts have shown up, too.
Colts have been started there
and loops from lariats have been thrown
While in between all that
old man winter's bitter wind has blown.
Sweat and blood have been shed there,
by both livestock and men...
Indeed, cattle and seasons have changed
alongside those old cow pens.

It's more than just a place
to work some cattle that were gathered...
It's also a place
where family, friends and cowhands meet and chatter.
Some feed's been poured to troughs there
and red whiskey into Dixie cups;

Fireside breakfasts have been had there
while the morning sun erupts.
And boy it sure looks pretty,
reminding you to say 'Amen',
As you're watching the breaking of the day
around those old cowpens.

They might hold weaned heifers
with fresh brands burned on their hides
Where kids saw their first heifer marked*
and it filled them up with pride.
They share a family's story there
on those seasoned cypress boards,
Through brands and names outlined,
inscribed by knife, and underscored.
A herding legacy passed on
thanks to their ancestral, sage cowmen,
Whose wisdom was handed down
while kids grew up inside those old cowpens.

During times when they sit empty,
overgrown with weeds and silence,
Ain't much better place to go
so as to clear your head and gain some sense.
Within their warm embrace,
they've seen homework done and Bibles read;
They've heard prayers whispered,
laughter shared and seen many a tear be shed.
More than wood, they're like a sacred hall
to be visited again and again.
No riches will buy the memories
that abide within those old cowpens.

* *Marked*: As in using a knife to cut/carve a person's ear mark into the ear of cattle. Individual earmarks vary and serve as a means for a man on horseback to quickly assess ownership of cattle from afar even when they can't see a brand.

A Bronco Meets Some Bulls

Traditionally, the tried and true crossbreeding program for cow/calf ranches in Florida revolved around a three breed rotation of Brahman, Hereford, and Angus yielding crossbred cattle best adapted to the harsh subtropical climate. Angus cattle are well-known for providing high quality carcass traits, Herefords are renowned for providing heavy bone structure and strong maternal traits while the Brahman breed provides heat tolerance and disease resistance such that a combination of these breeds provides cattle well-suited to their environment. The outcome of these crosses are Brangus or Braford crossbred cattle. Over the years, other more exotic breeds have been introduced and utilized in varying degrees but the genetic base for the cow herd is still predominately comprised of Brangus or Braford type cattle.

As is typical with bulls, they really don't want to have to move unless it's of their own accord. When you do get them moving they're still going to offer resistance or make every attempt to escape along the way, and the type of resistance they offer varies depending on the breed. For example in most cases, Brahman bulls are going to either fight you or they're going to try fleeing and hiding, Angus bulls will either jump belly deep into the nearest available water they can find or they'll pick a fight amongst other bulls to make things difficult, and Hereford bulls resist by simply taking their sweet time and slowing down the whole process of driving a group of cattle. Some days go easier than others.

On one particular morning of gathering bulls in preparation for the breeding season, it had been one-too-many long hot hours full of frustration in finding the bulls, pushing them from the mosaic of dense hammocks and marshes dotting the northwestern shoreline of Lake Okeechobee, and driving them across the prairie to the pens at Pearce Ranch. By the time they closed the gate behind the last bull into the pens, it was mid-morning and all those involved including bulls, cowboys, horses and dogs were hot and irritated.

The horses were watered, tied up under the shade of trees and then cinches on saddles were loosened. Everyone took a water break to cool off, stretch their legs and settle down. Well, almost everyone… Apparently, there was a small contingent that either hadn't had enough action or possibly had their irritation renewed upon entering the confinement of the pens; a handful of bulls who weren't quite ready to settle down. In particular, a couple of the more dominant, stronger bulls were fully engaged in a fight that showed no signs of stopping anytime soon. Dirt and dust rose in a cloud above the pens as the two of them circled with heads thrusting one against the other, all the while plowing into and through other bulls. While pushing and shoving each other across the pen from one side to the other some of the cypress boards bowed against their weight, echoed a loud cracking pop and splintered into pieces.

Things like that often happen in the pens and is to be expected when such large, powerful animals are placed in tight quarters. And most of the time, such skirmishes go ignored by the cowboys because the bulls settle on their own but this wasn't looking to be one of those occasions. By now, the escalating racket had drawn the crew's attention and everyone was attempting all the usual methods of distraction such as yelling, popping cow whips, chunking rocks to no avail. Big Daddy was sitting nearby and he'd had enough of those bulls tearing up the pens; it was simply more than he could stand. Ford had released their Bronco to compete against the Jeep and International Scout, both mainstays on Florida ranches back in the days prior to four wheel drive pickups and both of which Big Daddy had owned previously. His Bronco was outfitted with a cow-catcher on the front end and he was perfectly convinced that it was the answer to the bulls' problems that day.

As he turned the key and brought her to life he called out, "Boys, open up that gate and let me in there." As my dad recalls it, he cleared the gate and took a direct line right into the side of those two bulls and using the sturdy steel tubing of that cow-catcher started pushing them across the pen towards all the other bulls. Dad said that when the rear tires started to spin and lose traction against what amounted to a few tons of flesh, bone, and bad attitude, Big Daddy reached down onto the floorboard and grabbed a handful of that 4-wheel drive shifter and kept on shoving. A mix of dirt, small rocks, shell and recycled grass showered back away from the Bronco as the tires spun under the weight they were pushing.

What happened next was the coup de grâce on what had been a bad morning from the beginning.

As all four knobby mud tires on that Ford Bronco dug in, Big Daddy pinned the two instigators between him and the mob of innocent bovine bystanders cramming them tighter and tighter against the fence until something had to give. The poles and lumber were no match for all that pressure and the entire outer wall of the cow pens went down as every bull that had taken so much effort to get into the pens that morning scrambled off in a dozen different directions!

Glancing out from the driver's side window, Big Daddy looked at everyone and just as pleased with himself as could be, quipped something to the effect of how he had shown those damn bulls a thing or two so now everyone could go get 'em gathered back up. And my guess would be that after a few moments of wide-eyed astonishment coupled with heads shaking in discouragement, everybody set about fixing the pens before spending the remainder of the day gathering up those bulls once again. After all, they were aware of how things worked and this was another of those unwritten rules: nothing or nobody better tear up a man's cow pens, but it's perfectly fine for him to do it himself, and especially if done to prove a point.

A Come-To-Jesus Meeting on the Kissimmee

Sometimes the Celtic influences that run in the blood of Florida's oldest families are more easily seen and more readily identifiable than at other times. Long-time cowman and whip maker Junior Mills told of one such instance where those ancient character traits were on full display within my family one time while he was helping them pen a bunch of big steers at a place we called the Beef Pasture.

The place was so-named because in those days the steers were marketed much differently than they are today. In stark contrast to today's beef marketing scenario whereby calves are shipped at a much younger age and lighter weight headed to grow on high quality forage and then grains, back then the steers would be weaned off the cows and moved to this marshy piece of land lying on the southwesterly side of the Kissimmee River just before it reaches Lake Okeechobee. Once there, they would graze on the thick, fertile grass until they weighed 1,500 pounds or more before being shipped straight for beef.

Mr. Mills worked cattle all across Florida and he rode for many families in the lower Kissimmee River Valley at one time or another throughout the years. As he recalled, many days found him working on the Pearce cow crew riding the fertile, grassy prairies and low-lying peat bogs along the Kissimmee River; the kind of country that can make gathering and driving cattle painstakingly difficult and uniquely frustrating in many instances. Those challenges made up the downside of running cattle along the river, but they weren't enough to offset the tremendous advantages the terrain offered. Nature's pattern of seasonal flooding in these areas built up rich sandy-loam soils that were quite simply unparalleled for growing nutrient dense grass. And of course, that high quality forage in turn yielded fleshy, deep-bodied cattle which was precisely why all the steers went to the Beef Pasture.

If you could ever get all the cattle pushed out from the marshes and glades along the river and onto the open prairie, then handling them-driving and penning them-got a whole lot easier. There wasn't a clear transition from pasture to open water on the river, but rather it was then, and in some areas today still is, a transitional area of bottomlands dotted with scattered trees and thick brush and alternating high and low ground. Depending on the time of year and the amount of rainfall, someone hunting cows in that area might encounter a large number of isolated high spots or small islands providing respite from the water for cattle and wildlife alike. While he didn't recall the exact year, Junior Mills recounted one time in particular where the highlight of the day happened on one of those river islands while working on the Pearce cow crew with J.O. Pearce, Sr, J.O. Pearce, Jr, and Forrest "Hunky" Pearce.

The plan for the day was to "gather the Beef Pasture" and get the steers which were heavy enough hauled to market. To begin, they would ride away from the pens to the farthest corners of the pasture at which time the riders would fan out sweeping an arc across the remainder of the pasture. In doing so, they'd be locating and picking up the cattle as they went and work on pushing them from the brush out to an open area where they'd "bunch 'em up" before driving them to the cow pens. Factoring in the topography of the land coupled with knowing the habits of the cattle, the most efficient route for driving the herd is established and repetitively used each time for that herd. The bovine species can be a complete conundrum because one minute they'll have you thinking them to be the dumbest animal on the face of God's green Earth and the next moment they'll amaze you with some movement or action implying a near-cognitive thinking process.

Such was the case of gathering these big steers at the Beef Pasture because according to Mr. Mills, who was intimately familiar with this piece of land from having worked for my family on a regular basis, there was one specific spot where one of those steers would make his escape each and every time these cattle were worked. It seems as though each time the cow crew passed this particular locale near a fairly large island, it was like clockwork for this big ole steer to quit the herd, run in a full sprint towards the water where he'd leap into the air and hit it like an olympic swimmer making his way to that island where he'd then crawl onto the muddy bank and disappear into the trees. Mr. Mills didn't know the exact number of times this steer had successfully pulled of this Houdini act; he allowed that it must have been quite a few because the steer was significantly bigger than any of the other steers in the group and well overdue to get run through the market, but the balance of power was getting ready to shift and the status quo was about to change.

As that one steer made his run for the old river bottom, the procession of men, cattle and horses paused momentarily as everyone watched the events unfold. Everyone paused that is except for Hunky Pearce. He stepped down from his horse and started pulling clothes off. Big Daddy (J.O. Pearce, Sr) squinted quizzically and asked him just what he thought he was doing. Hunky had seen that steer run off time and time again and was at the point he couldn't stand it any longer. He looked up at Big Daddy and replied, "Daddy, just sit right there and wait a minute and I'll show you." As Hunky's intentions became clear, Big Daddy tried talking him out of it and told him to get back on his horse, but thanks to those residual qualities of the Celtic temperament-stubbornness, an unwillingness to do anything by half-measure, and an unyielding determination-there wasn't any chance of dissuading him in his plans. Hunky argued that the steer had done that little trick way too many times, how he was way bigger than all the rest of them and it was well past time for him to leave. And with that, Hunky finished pulling off the last stitch of clothes he had on and waded into the water naked as a jaybird!

(L - R) J.O. Pearce, Jr, J.O. Pearce, Sr, and Forrest "Hunky" Pearce leaning on one of the Jeeps that provided the earliest means of 4x4 transportation in Florida's marshy cow country.

Everyone just settled in their saddles waiting to see what kind of show was about to unfold before their eyes. Emerging from the water onto the island, Hunky walked over to the first willow tree he saw and proceeded to break off the biggest branch he could get. Now mind you, none of the Pearce men were small and Hunky stood somewhere in the neighborhood of 6'4" and was probably on the upper side of 250 pounds so what he tore off that willow tree was a good-sized hunk of wood and not just a little twig or flimsy switch. Newly acquired club in hand and bare-assed, he disappeared into the woods.

For a short time there was silence, and then it was abruptly broken as all hell broke loose. Mr. Mills said the biggest bunch of racket and commotion you'd ever want to hear broke loose, rising from the trees on that island and echoing across the water. It was a mixture of Hunky's yelling and hollering along with the steer's bellowing, bawling, and snorting. Tree limbs were visibly shaking, waving back and forth, and you could hear them snapping and crashing. This continued for several minutes until suddenly the big Brahman-cross steer came busting out of the underbrush, hit the water like a torpedo and scrambled back onto the mainland then darted back into that bunch of cattle quick as lightning!

There's no way to have known whether the incident was a permanent reminder for that steer to avoid trying the island escape again because he was never given the opportunity to think about it anymore. Once he was back in the bunch and Hunky was clothed and back in the saddle, the crew finished driving them to the pens and the troublemaker took a ride to the market.

Looking Past the Laughter

If we briefly set aside the obvious humor found in the previous two stories, there's a subtle, yet larger context revealed in these encounters; it's one that could easily be overlooked, but serves as a brilliant illustration if we're willing to look deeper. The small nuance of which I speak is the fact that the sheer force of will displayed by the Pearce men and so many other pioneer families of Florida like them, a trait passed through the bloodline from Celtic ancestors across the eons, is the very same force that contributed so greatly to forging a state from a territory where others had failed. Granted, as much as it worked in their favor, that bullheadedness and dogged-determination to exert their will was a double-edged sword and could work against them just as quickly (like when Big Daddy accidentally pushed down an entire wall of the cow pens).

Pioneer families in Florida were driven by the same ethos predominant amongst their Gaelic and Celtic Briton forebears back in their ancestral homelands. It's a psyche rooted in steadfast loyalty, fierce independence, and an unyielding fortitude in the face of adversities or potentially insurmountable obstacles. Few other men and women could have been more ideally suited to surviving in the harsh climate and unforgiving wilds of territorial Florida. Rather than just surviving, these sturdy settlers went on to thrive and created a cattle legacy that endures to this day.

These Scots-Irish families played as hard as they worked and to be honest, the two activities usually happened congruently with one another. From old cowhunters to the hired cowboys, sharing jokes, pulling pranks and generally cuttin' the fool were then, and have remained to this day, commonplace pastimes that helped lighten the mood and make the time pass by more quickly.

May good luck be your friend in whatever you do and may trouble be always a stranger to you.

~ Gaelic Blessing

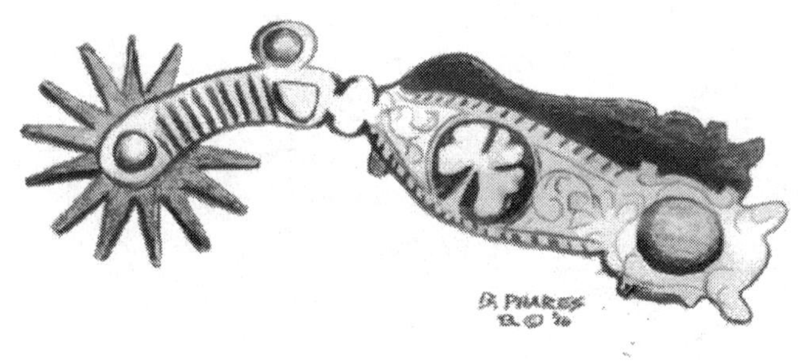

The Ever-Versatile and Not-So-Pretty Ranch Truck

Every ranch family I've ever known has one cruising around their property somewhere… that beat up, worn out pile of metal and rubber that vaguely resembles a truck. Most often, this slow rolling beauty belongs to the patriarch of the family, as it seems to be a rite of passage when they assume that role in life. Much like a king receives the crown and scepter in monarchial societies to symbolize their position of rule, proudly driving crinkled sheet metal seems to be the insignia of choice in the ranching world.

Though each ranch truck may differ slightly in appearance, they all share certain common elements. Invariably, they are riddled with dents, dings and scratches from the front bumper to the rear and all points in between. From raking limbs down the sides of the truck to using it as a means of offering a "friendly shove" to an unruly bovine, that shiny new showroom finish never lasts long. As a matter of fact, I've been told that one man was known to take a ball-peen hammer and knock a huge dent in his tailgate the day he bought his truck! His theory was that something was going to happen to it eventually so it just as well happen sooner versus later so he didn't have to worry about "babying" his new truck. They are put into action to get ranch work done by whatever means necessary and this dimpled appearance is most often the result of the ways in which they end up becoming a cowboy's biggest tool more so than their originally intended use a means of conveyance.

If it's the rainy season they're coated in mud, and if it's dry they'll have a protective film of dust layered thick over the metallic paint. The bed of these trucks is usually littered with hand tools, chains, empty cans, cattle medicine bottles, chains, rope, rolls of barbed-wire and Lord only knows what other miscellaneous items. The ranch truck is indeed a multi-functional vehicle that gets used and abused like no other. They are the cattleman's office on wheels and his shipping mechanism to get livestock hauled or supplies to the ranch. They can be a tour bus for city folk who've come to visit or a classroom for the younger generation of the family as they learn the ranching business.

Though it may seem pretty strange today, back before gooseneck trailers got a lot of use in Florida, it was not uncommon to see cowboys hauling their horses in the back of their pickup surrounded by a metal rack. They'd find a spot to back the truck into a ditch where the horses didn't have to jump so high to get loaded in the bed of the truck.

Beyond the dented exterior, another typical feature of these trucks is their less than immaculate interior wherein they will have at minimum, a good half-inch layer of dirt, cow manure, and grass in the floorboard area. And very likely, that mixture on the floor will have crumbs or some other sort of food material sprinkled in for good measure. Before extended cab and 4-door trucks gained popularity, the dashboard was the catch-all shelf, the "junk drawer" of the truck, if you will. It held livestock feed receipts, fuel tickets, animal medication label instructions–all of these printed on paper colored in more shades than can be found in a rainbow–along with empty brown paper sacks, aspirin bottles, Hot Shot cattle prods accompanied by a few dozen of their replacement batteries rolling about loosely amongst the other junk, ear tags, ink pens, tattoo ink, possibly a knife, and probably a couple packs of cheese and peanut butter crackers, beanie-weenies, canned corned beef or sardines. Depending on the year, make and model of the truck, the dash might have been too sloped or too narrow to hold everything causing it to constantly fall into the floor. The same gentleman who employed the ball-peen hammer philosophy found a cure for this problem by screwing a 2×4 onto his dash to make a lip that kept everything up there where it belonged...

I have fond memories of me and my two brothers all crammed onto the seat together riding shotgun with Grandaddy. We were short enough that we could hardly see over all the junk piled up on his dash and Lord help us if he took to chasing across the pasture after cattle and hit a hole because while we hit our heads ricocheting off the window or ceiling, all that stuff on the dash was levitating into the air as well and ended up in our laps when our fannies found the seat once again. When we were too young to ride horseback gathering cattle we rode in the truck with Grandaddy because he no longer rode horseback either, having fallen victim of too many horse wrecks resulting in bad knees. In particular, I remember being in the back of the truck braced up and peering over the cab while racing ahead of everyone else riding horseback and driving the cattle. Our job was to reach and open a barbed-wire gap ahead of them for a cow or bull that they had managed to single out of the herd for some reason that I don't recall now. As grandaddy hit the brakes when we neared the wire gate, they locked up on the wet grass and the sliding truck continued speeding ahead. Too close to do anything different, he hollered out the window for us to get down. We dropped into a crouch just in time to see the wire go flying over the both the truck cab and us kids as we slid right through the middle of it busting it to pieces. Gliding to a stop, Grandaddy leaned out of his window and said, "I guess we got that one opened up, didn't we?"

My mom and dad have memories and stories of my great grandfather's Jeeps, Scouts and Broncos that he drove on the ranch, I have these memories of Grandaddy's trucks, and my kids are building memories of my dad's truck each day.

I can vividly recall another one of my Grandad's trucks that we affectionately referred to as "old scratch and dent". I can still picture every detail of it to this day. It was a single cab, early to mid 80's model Ford that was two-tone black on silver in color. A metal antenna about 2 feet in length and used for the Motorola two-way radio protruded from the top of the cab and as we drove under any low hanging oak limbs on the ranch, it would clamor and clang against the cab as it flexed to and fro on its spring base. That radio unit sat mounted near our feet inside the cab.

On the outer shell of the driver's side door, there was a large, half-moon shaped area that was primer gray and devoid of any paint. This area was polished smooth and glossy from his left elbow rubbing back and forth where he always leaned towards the door with that arm partially out the window as he rode around the ranch checking on cows or all of us working. Being diabetic, Grandaddy for years drank TAB when it was the only diet cola and the cans would be heaped in what to us kids seemed like a mountainous pile in the back of that truck until he'd finally decide that we should clean them out. Just as clearly as if I were sitting in that truck with him now, I can see him with his head tilted back draining the last drops with that little shake of the can he always did before pulling it from his lips and pinching it once in the middle so it wouldn't roll around then he'd extend his arm out the window and backhand toss it to the bed of the truck.

Some, or all, of the previously mentioned items were piled on the dash… dirt was in the floor… cow manure was splattered across the fender wells from mud grip tires… and his love for us, the land and the lifestyle filled that truck to overflowing. With a little bit of luck and the good Lord's blessing, I'll get to offer that to some grandkids of my own one of these days.

And ranch trucks don't have to be road ready or functional to benefit a ranch. Sometimes they are simply visual reminders of family and days gone by. For example, one evening as daylight was quickly fading while I was finishing up chores before heading in for supper, I stopped to snap some photos of a big thunderhead coming across Lake Okeechobee and rolling in our direction. The twilight shadows made it look heavier and more ominous than it really was, and the setting sun brilliantly highlighted the top of it in sharp contrast to everything else. The horses grazing quietly in the foreground added to the composition and although my iPhone was the only camera I had close at hand, I could still grab some nice shots (as an artist, I'm always taking photos for painting reference or ideas to spark new pieces of work). After grabbing a few quick shots, I turned back to the work I needed to finish. As I came out of the barn, I happened to glance to the west and realized that the sky was lit up as if it was on fire. After retrieving my Canon camera, I quickly started snapping off photos.

As I framed up the shots, something in the distance caught my attention. One of my granddaddy's old trucks, a late 70's model Ford F-150 that was powder blue with a white cab was sitting there by our cowpens silhouetted against that awe-inspiring skyline of glowing pastel oranges, pinks, and purples overlaid against a backdrop shaded in turquoise and blue. That old truck has been sitting there waiting for new bearings in the front for quite a while, but on that particular evening its function was to serve as the subject matter for some nice photos. With full knowledge that the colors and my opportunity would be rapidly deteriorating, I quickly walked across the pasture to where the old truck sat next to piles of fence posts and culverts. I made it just in time to grab some really nice shots and recall some fond memories in the process.

The old Ford has changed a lot over the years since Granddaddy had it and hauled us around in it. As a matter of fact, when finished with truck he sold it to Mike Spires, known more affectionately to most of us as "Pansy," for use as a work truck. Mike had spent many years dayworking cattle and building fence for us and I can remember being a youngster looking up to him, his brother Robbie and many of the others who helped us at the ranch. Mike converted the truck to a standard transmission, put a flatbed on the back and a cow catcher on the front end. The old truck had changed hands another time or two before mom had the chance to buy it back one day with the intentions of her being able to leave it at the ranch where she could park her car and use the truck to ride through the cows every now and then.

I can't look at that truck without thinking of all the early mornings my brothers and I would pile onto the big bench seat and peer over the dashboard full of feed tickets, receipts for cow medicines, plastic boxes of .22LR ammo, Hot Shot batteries, aspirin bottles and more as we drove around to the Phillips 66 gas station on US Hwy 441, locally known as South Parrott Avenue, where J.W. Pope would come out to fill us up, wash the windshield, and so forth before we headed to the ranch with Granddaddy. It was your typical gas station for that time period. Aside from the service islands with gas pumps, there were two service bays to the south side of the building and on the north end, there was a small office space where a single, paper-covered desk and chair sat to one side of the room against plate glass windows while tires sat perched in a row around the top shelf of the room accompanied by belts and other miscellaneous parts hanging from the ceiling. Shelves with batteries and more parts lined the lower half of the opposite wall.

Granddaddy would always let us go inside for drinks and snacks. Given the limited space, the choices were surprisingly numerous. As you entered the narrow front doorway, the bottom shelf at your feet and to the left was a veritable smorgasbord of candy, gum, crackers, Moonpies and the like. The snack decisions we faced were monumental…at least they were in a kids' mind. For candy, would it be a bar or packaged candy like M&M's or Sixlets? Would we get SuperBubble in original or green apple flavor for 5 cents a piece or the old favorite, Juicy Fruit? Did we want Tom's Crackers or a Moon Pie, and if it was a Moon Pie, chocolate or banana flavor? Nearby, a Coca-Cola drink machine dispensed 16 oz glass bottles, Nehi Peach drinks, and Yoo-hoo's in the smaller glass bottles…and all of them required a bottle opener to remove the bottle caps. Occasionally, one of us would forget to pop the top from our bottle before leaving and we'd sit in the truck mystified as Granddaddy would pull his pocketknife from his right front pants pocket catching the crimped edge of the cap with the closed butt end of that knife then effortlessly flip it into the air. There was an art to it, and he taught us how to do it well.

And then there's the morning I learned my biggest lesson in gun safety the hard way, right there at those gas pumps… Like Ralphie from the movie "A Christmas Story," my brother Brian and I had just gotten brand new Red Ryder BB guns and we were wound up like an eight day clock at the prospect of using them to chase any animal that moved down at the ranch that particular day. In fact, they were so new and we were so inexperienced with them that we didn't yet understand all aspects of the BB guns even though my dad had already preached and demonstrated gun safety to us several times over. Having already grabbed our drinks and snacks, we hopped into the truck and picked up our BB guns while waiting for Granddaddy to get back in with us.

As he slid behind the wheel, he glanced my way noticing that instead of having the barrel of the gun pointed to the floor, I had it pointed at the back edge of the cab roof instead of the floorboard. Additionally, my 7 year old brain for some reason told my finger that it should be resting on the trigger. Now, everyone knows that you never place your finger on the trigger until you're on target and ready to shoot. Granddaddy looked at me and told me that I ought not have my finger on the trigger to which I replied, "But, it's on safety Granddaddy, see?" at which point I squeezed the trigger and shot out the cab dome light! Before I knew what had happened, and while I sat in complete disbelief, Granddaddy reached over and thumped me on the top of my head so hard that I was still rubbing it a couple hours later. I don't remember him saying a word to me; it was just that hammering thump to my head that drove home a point that has remained with me to this day.

You know what else is still around to this day? In spite of ownership changes, new parts for the truck, and roughly thirty-five years, that original shot-out dome light is still in the roof of that old blue truck. In setting out to capture some new memories with the camera, that afternoon I also stirred up a whole lot of old ones in the process. Just as the setting sun paints the evening sky, memories like these color our lives, growing sweeter and more nostalgic each time they rise and set in our minds.

"A good tale never tires in the telling."
- Scottish Proverb

Celtic Influences on the Creek Nation and Beyond

With Colonial America's presence ever-looming and expanding further into the backcountry regions that were home to native tribes, ensuing clashes were inevitable. Oddly enough, these clashes were often between two groups with much more in common than either of them knew: both groups had origins as tribal societies, both placed a premium on personal liberty, both were rooted in a warrior ethos, and ironically enough the Scots-Irish were now encroaching and displacing American tribes after having themselves quite often been expelled by force from their ancestral homelands at the hands of Britain.

Still, in many cases mutually peaceful relationships thrived and resulted in a large volume of trade between the two cultures. Such was the case along the coastal floodplains of Georgia where in the 1730's, British philanthropist James Oglethorpe founded the city of Savannah by enticing a band of Highlanders from the Inverness region of Scotland to settle the area with aspirations that this Presbyterian group would act as a buffering mechanism against the Catholic Spanish in Florida. From within this population, Clan Chattan was the nearly exclusive trading partner within the Creek nation. The overwhelmingly most sought after trade item was cloth for a kilt because conveniently and coincidentally enough, the Scottish kilt which had been outlawed by the British upon their final defeat of the Scots at Culloden, very much resembled the traditional male Creek breechcloth. The two similar outfits proved to be especially suitable for the wet, boggy marshes of the coastal plains and the interior swamps of Georgia. At one point, traveler William Bartram even wrote of his own observation likening Creek dress to the highland kilt. Early traders of Scottish origin also impacted Creek headdress by selling a number of turban like coverings, most often woolen shawls, to which the Seminoles would often adorn with feathers to further compliment the cloth's appearance, ostrich plumes being the preferred choice followed by egret plumes.

In the face of mounting pressure, encroachment, and conflicts, Creeks fled south into the interior reaches of Florida by the thousands where they would assimilate with descendants of many other tribes such as Hitchiti, Apalachee, Miccosuki, Yemassee, Yuchi, Tequesta, Apalachicola, Choctaw, and Oconee. This commingling of tribes formed the nucleus of today's Seminole Tribe of Florida and as they continued to migrate southward down the Florida peninsula they carried with them the seeds of Celtic influence reflected in their clothing, genetics (resulting from marriages between Scots traders and native women), and perhaps most importantly an appreciation for cattle herding.

As mentioned earlier, Florida's native culture was for many years the primary herding society on the peninsula. Throughout many years they had taken advantage of the livestock which the Spanish had given such little attention and slowly amassed herds numbering in the thousands. In fact by the mid 1700's, Oconee Creek leader, Cowkeeper, and his followers had established a vast settlement in the Alachua area where on and around Paynes Prairie their herds increased to somewhere between 7,000 to 10,000 head. Even at that early time, they were said to work these cattle with trained cow dogs.

Cattle raising for the Seminoles dwindled following the Second (1835-1842) and Third Seminole Wars (1855-1858) and the tribe's herding heritage was not revived until the 1930's when substandard starter herds were acquired from the federal government. Widely known as being excellent cattlemen, the Seminoles exercised good stewardship over the herds eventually growing to be one of the largest cow/calf operations in America today. The Tribe's vision for the future and vibrant spirit has helped them expand their cattle operations to include Seminole Pride branded beef and an affiliated seedstock operation, Salacoa Valley Farms, in Georgia.

Fub le che cho bee: Ode to the Big Wind

Preface: The Seminole Tribe of Florida's rich history and cultural tradition captivated me from an early age and ranching between Lake Okeechobee and the Brighton Seminole Reservation proves to be a constant source of inspiration for not only my oil paintings but for my writing as well. I try hard not to miss an opportunity to hear firsthand or read of their legends and stories that have been passed down through the years.

After recently stumbling upon a story by Mrs. Betty Mae Jumper and another short story by Mr. James E. Billie, Chairman of the Seminole Tribe of Florida, the images they painted in my mind with their words began to take root in the form of a few rhyming lines that persisted, begging to flow out of my head and onto paper. I turned to several of my friends in the Brighton and Hollywood communities to clarify the meaning and pronunciation of words–some in Miccosukee and others in the Creek language and I'm ever-grateful for them entertaining my curiosity once more.

As a cursory introduction, most Floridians are all too familiar with hurricanes and in today's information age there's plenty of advance notice as to when one is heading your way as well as its intensity. In the bygone days of old Florida, there were none of the mass communicated warnings like we have today and the Seminoles relied on other means to know when hurricanes or tropical storms were coming. However, Seminole lore holds that the Big Wind, Fub le che cho bee (pronounced with a long E sound) or Ho-tale-tha-ko depending on the language, is a woman who lost her child and is searching for it. As she passes by, you are not supposed to blow on anything that will make a sharp whistling noise because this will sound like her lost baby and cause her to come towards you with great force in an effort to save her child.

In lieu of today's technology, the old method of gauging the intensity of Big Wind whenever she approached was to look for the "hurricane bird," the Swallow-tailed Kite. They migrate to Florida each year just prior to the onset of hurricane season and nest here throughout the summer and fall. Once they had an indication of Big Wind's strength, as a means of seeking protection for their chickees/houses and their families, tribal members can seek help from members belonging to the Wind Clan and/or they can place an object such as an ax, knife, or machete standing in the ground with its sharp edge facing the direction from which the Big Wind is coming causing it to divide and go around without causing any destruction.

The number 4 is of significance in many native cultures and medicine so 4 sharp edges towards Big Wind holds stronger medicine and offers more protection.

With all that said, and acknowledging that I've likely overlooked some details in setting the stage for this poem, here it is with my hope that you enjoy it while learning a little more Florida history.

When summer and fall roll in,
Steamy Florida days
Succumb to shifting winds
Sweeping over the glades,
Into pine and oaks
And through the cypress trees…
Tickling the palmettos;
Swirling across the prairies.

Seminole elders tell kids
Don't make no whistling sounds;
No blowing flutes or bottles…
Don't y'all be messing around.
'Cause Big Wind she's listening,
Searching for her baby's cry
And if she hears your noise
She's sure to come blowing by

Fub le che cho bee
Season of strong wind
Fub le che cho bee
Big Wind blowing in

See the hurricane bird
Gliding in the sky…
Does he circle down low
Or does he soar up high?
Follow his forked tail,
Learn to read the signs
For gauging strength of storms,
The Kite tells no lies

Then observe the clouds
And once you've made your scan
It's time to ask for help
From members of Wind Clan*
They'll speak up for you
And share an earnest plea
Calling on Big Wind
To spare your chickee

Fub le che cho bee
Season of strong wind
Fub le che cho bee
Big Wind blowing in

Ax, machete or knife
Planted in the ground
With sharp side to Big Wind
Splits her…makes her go around.
If she's really angry
With a voice that roars
Make it even stronger

Lining them up in fours.

If she comes anyway,
Slide the chickee* roof down,
With everyone safe beneath
As it sits flat on the ground.
Soon her natural course,
Sends her further on somewhere.
Leaving behind blue skies
With lots of pure, clean air.

Fub le che cho bee
Season of strong wind
Fub le che cho bee
Big Wind blowing in
Farewell, Fub le che cho bee…
Until you come back again.

* *Wind Clan*: in the Seminole culture, clans are extended family units represented by a non-human entity and each clan is characterized by the traits it shares with that non-human entity, such as strength, courage, knowledge, etc. The eight Seminole clans are: Panther, Bear, Deer, Bird, Snake, Otter, Bigtown, and Wind.

* Chickee: an open-sided dwelling having a roof thatched from fronds of the sabal or "cabbage" palm. The uprights and supporting structure of the roof are typically made from cypress poles and limbs.

Chapter 3

Ranch Raised

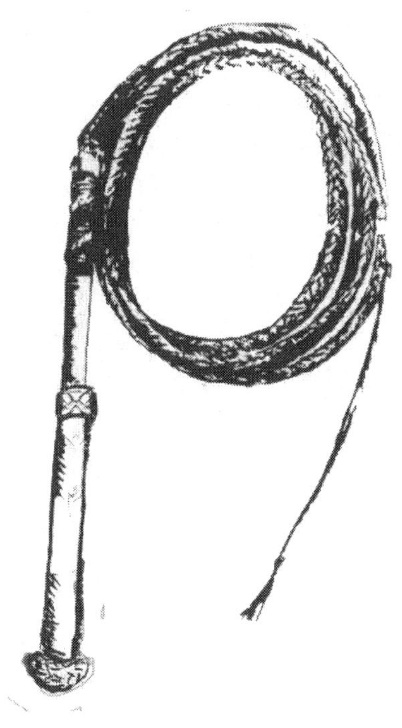

You'll Always Remember the Ride

This poem was written on the occasion of my Grandaddy's passing in 1997. It speaks to his character and all the things that he was to his family.

You'll always remember the ride you shared,
Taking you 'cross lush prairies and boggy sloughs*.
But the tough times didn't matter much,
Cause this cowman had wits enough to pull you through.
He was strong, hardworking
And you loved the way he lived–
Flashing everyone that warm smile,
Always looking to see what of himself he could give.

This cowman lived for the land and animals,
Making sure on you this passion he'd impart.
Sunrises and raindrops hitting the grass…
Nature's simplicities always brought joy into his heart.
Besides the range and cattle,
He knew the ways of his fellow man.
Time and again his example proved
That actions speak louder than any word can.

T'was many a lesson for him to share,
And amazing to you, was the breadth of wisdom within his brow.
From building a fence to cuttin' a cabbage*,
He showed you how to sit a horse
And have a good eye for cows.
In life's work he never dabbled,
He was born a hard worker and gave it all he had
But when there was time to play,
Your friend was more than ready to laugh and be glad.

Now one of the best cowmen's been called home,
'Cause the Lord's herds grow fast and he gets short a hand or two.
Your partner's gone on ahead,
To scout the way and fix a place for you.
And you'll always remember the ride,
Knowing one day it's gonna continue.
Your cowman's got one eye on the Savior's herd
And one on those he entrusted to you.

* *Slough:* low-lying, wet areas typically found throughout Florida's rangelands.

* *Cuttin' a cabbage*: referes to cutting down a Sabal Palm tree, more commonly referred to by native Floridians as a "cabbage tree" in order to get the heart of palm for cooking a dish known as "swamp cabbage"

A Cowman's Angel

I wrote this poem upon the passing of my Granny, Marian Pearce, and dedicated it to her on March 6, 2007.

She was born to be a cowman's angel
Though she never knew as much
When she was just a little girl
Having tea with her dolls and such
Then, as a young woman, that moment came
When out of the blue, and quite by surprise,
That confident and handsome cowman
Stole her heart when he caught her eye
And each of us has a calling–
A special gift to be used in a particular place
And her place happened to be on the prairie
Providing a family with comfort, love and grace

As a cowman's angel on the prairie,
Both her love and duties knew no bounds.
She'd do anything from tending livestock,
To keeping the books and runnin' errands around town.
This lady of mercy sacrificed herself-
She washed, cleaned and toiled without a fuss.
Why she even made the time
To go with the kids for field trips on the bus.
And when it was time to round-up cattle,
She'd rise before the sun to start the meal for noon
Cookin' all the morning through,
She'd fill her motorized dinner wagon and bring lunch out to the crew.

Yes, she was born to be a cowman's angel
And now her earthly work is through.
Her handsome cowman rode ahead ten years ago-
Now it's time for her to follow him and go home, too.
How we'll miss her kind and gentle ways,
The soft comfort of her warm embrace,
The tenderness of her voice,
And the shining light from her sweet face.
Our loss has been the Master's gain,
Yet she looks down upon the prairie and guides us still
As we carry her loving example forward,
Through the virtues in our hearts which she instilled.

Granny's Dinner Wagon

One of the most indelible memories I hold from my childhood, and I'm sure my brothers would agree, is that of my Granny bringing dinner out to the cow crew at the ranch each day around the noon hour. Of course my brothers and I were still in school most of the time, so the memories I recall are of these hot dinners served up during the sweltering summer days we'd spend working with our cousins. And lest you think I'm crazy, I did in fact mean to say dinner versus lunch. For those less fortunate souls unfamiliar with Southern culture, the noon meal is dinner and the evening meal is supper.

My Granny, Marian Dillard Pearce, grew up in Washington, North Carolina near the Outer Banks coastal region. When Granddaddy was younger, he worked for a road construction company to supplement his income as he was building his cattle herd and he met Granny while working on a project in North Carolina. As a young lady, her blue eyes, framed by wavy locks of shoulder length black hair, sparkled brilliantly as they still did beneath her glasses when she watched us grow up and bring her great-grandchildren by for a visit. And I'm quite certain, that as a young lady having grown up near the Outer Banks, she had to do a lot of adapting when she married into the cattle ranching business and moved to Okeechobee, Florida.

Most married couples–and especially those who work together in business–tend to have an occasional disagreement, but I don't ever remember one instance where Granddaddy and Granny ever showed the first sign of quarreling with each other. As family trees grow and branches split off in all directions, so do the business interests. As mentioned earlier, in the beginning years of their marriage, the family ranching operation still existed along with Granddaddy having his own cattle and eventually some of his own land. While growing up I remember Granny keeping the books for Granddaddy's personal cattle, the ranch corporation and keeping the meals rolling out of that kitchen.

Like they do for most any ranching family, the day would always start before sunrise. While Granddaddy was not a coffee drinker, each morning he would get up and start the coffee for Granny so that when she came into the kitchen to start preparing dinner for the crew, fresh hot coffee was awaiting her. Granny would spend the entire morning chopping, peeling, mixing, stirring and pouring herself into all that food in the kitchen before loading it into the cavernous trunk of her car for the trip out to the ranch. Granny drove a Mercury Grand Marquis and this was back in the day when nearly every American car was HUGE. This thing was built like a WWII-era Sherman tank… I swear, it seemed like I could have run laps in the rear floorboard space when riding in it. Of course, seat belts weren't required by law back then so if you got tired and wanted a little cat nap, then you simply climbed up onto the bench-like shelf between the rear windshield and the rear seat to sprawl out! Loading the vehicle down with all the food was no problem and once it was in there, plenty of space for passengers was still available.

Before two-way radios and cell phones were around to aid in communication, the cow crew basically planned to find a stopping point in the cow work as close to noon as possible, or as was more often the case, they might even just keep working right up until they could see the sun glinting off the windshield of that big blue car as it came along the dirt road leading across the wide open prairie and back to the pens. She was often spotted as she turned off the highway and came through the gate by the hungriest in the crew that day and at that point, you'd hear someone shout "The dinner wagon's here!"

Dayworkers and family members would then find a water trough or cooler to wash up their face and hands before forming a semi-circle at the back of her car as she popped the trunk under the shade of a tree or barn. Someone would grab the cooler full of sweet tea while another would grab the cooler of ice and everyone else would search for any other items left to carry. On occasion, the pots and pans full of food would be carried to another location for serving, but most often, the huge trunk space would double as a buffet line with everyone filing by to pile up their plates with Granny's delicious southern cooking that she somehow managed to keep piping hot upon arrival. The main dish might be country fried steak, beef roast, beef tips, meatloaf and either rice or mashed potatoes – both served with some good brown gravy and all accompanied by side dishes like cow peas [crowder peas], green beans, made-from-scratch Mac & Cheese, collard greens and a big brown paper grocery sack full of biscuits.

Stories of the day along with a few jokes would be exchanged and pranks would be pulled as everyone gathered together over the meal. We'd all go back for second helpings and dessert, eating way more than what was prudent for anyone having to go back to work again. Next, we'd help get everything loaded back into the car so Granny could go on back to town and deal with any banking or bookkeeping plus begin to prepare supper. Once that was done, we'd pile up for a sweaty nap in the sticky midday heat if there was time to squeeze one in.

Everyone loved Granny's cooking and looked forward to it each day. If Hobart Lee was working for us, you'd be apt to catch him later in the day perched atop his horse with another biscuit in hand and another two or three in his pocket after having eaten at least that many with his dinner.

Nothing remains the same forever. As with all good things, the end of Granny's dinner wagon came too soon... Not due to her inability to prepare it, but rather due to changing times and priorities. The dayworkers got their heads together and decided that a raise in wages across the region was in order. They wound up getting a few extra dollars per day but lost a hot, home cooked meal in the process. Having dayworked throughout South Florida myself, I've been on both sides of this issue, and in my opinion, I'd rather have a good meal than an extra $5 -$10 per day and a cold bologna sandwich. Although those elaborate dinnertime meals have long since passed by, mentally, I still savor them and relish in the memory of those bygone days.

She's As Pretty as the Morning

She's as pretty as the morning
  when the sun gives you its first glance.
This woman clings to you,
  your life ever longer to enhance.

Like the dawning of each day
  giving chase to shadows of the night,
She helps you to envision
  ideas and dreams hidden from your sight.

With the warmth of a summer dawn,
  she wraps her love around your heart.
And you come to know that feeling,
  is one with which you just can't part.

She's as pretty as the morning
  when the grass is shining in the dew.
Just her laughter and her smile
  makes the routine things seem new.

Like an early winter's morn
  with coolness heavy in the air,
Her soothing and quiet ways
  instill an easiness everywhere.

There's something about daybreak
  that grasps and envelopes you whole.
So does this lovely lady
  capture your spirit and fill your soul.

She's as pretty as the morning,
 and each one she'll share at your side.
You're blessed to have this woman–
 your lifelong companion and bride.

Pointing Towards the Past

Most Florida ranchers are completely unaware of another simple, yet highly symbolic connection between their ancestral roots and their present day lives: the Thistle plant.

Oddly enough, this lowly, humble weed that is most often viewed as a nuisance in the pasture due to the fact it can potentially disrupt grazing if left unchecked is actually the national emblem of Scotland. While there are many legends surrounding its origin as the Scottish national emblem, the most popular stems from the 13th century when Norsemen under the leadership of King Haakon attempting to conquer the Scots suffered gales and fierce storms becoming beached at Largs in Ayrshire. According to legend, the Norwegian forces decided they would attempt to surprise the sleeping Scottish clansmen and as a manner of stealth in the cover of darkness, they removed their footwear. As they crept barefoot advancing on the Scots position, they unknowingly encountered an area of ground covered with a dense patch of thistles at which point one of Haakon's men stepped on one of the spiny plants shrieking in pain. Alerted to the position of the advancing Norsemen, the clansmen plunged into what became known as the Battle of Largs where Haakon was defeated thus saving Scotland from invasion. The thistle's important role in these events was recognized and thus it was chosen as the national emblem.

Other than the fact that the thistle grows both in Florida and Scotland, there are numerous similarities lending themselves to an intriguing love-hate relationship between this plant and Florida's Scots-Irish families. Momentarily laying aside the idea that thistles are nothing more than a weed to control in the pasture, the most strikingly similar trait shared by both Florida cowhunters and the thistle lies in their hardiness and resilience to adversity. Thriving in Florida's harsh climate is no easy feat, but thanks to their stubborn nature Florida ranchers and the thistle plant continue to persevere. Furthermore, both the plant and the people have a tough exterior shell to protect their beautiful and vibrant interior components: the flower blossoms for the plants and warm, kind-hearted souls in the case of the people.

An old Gaelic proverb wisely proclaims, *"Danger and delight grow on one stalk."* Perhaps, the thistle was the inspiration behind these prudent words? The admonishment is easily self-applicable as a reminder to loved ones that unseen threats are ever-present, but it's also a very shrewd warning to others that behind the warm, fun-loving side of Scots-Irishmen the underpinnings of a fierce and formidable foe lay hidden unless and until needed.

Now, by no means am I suggesting that thistle plants should be left to spread freely across Florida pasturelands. Thistles in large quantities can easily inhibit the growth of quality forages for cattle on the ranch, but at the same time the historical background of the plant does cast an interesting context on Florida ranch lands and serves as a subtle reminder of the ancestral roots so many of us share.

Rearview Reflections

Cool air sinks and settles in
Below a fiery sky at the end of day
And another year of living
Falls behind him and quietly rolls away.
He rambles across the ranch
Riding alone and taking in the view
Including his own reflection–
Stubble shaded white and gray, eyes of squinted blue
There's been high's and low's
In the first forty-some-odd years he's had
And when everything's been tallied
He recalls seeing more of the good life than the bad
It's all there written on his face
As crows' feet crease and run a little deeper
This old world keeps turning faster
Making the cost of livin' none the cheaper.

Amidst the change core values remain...
Maxims instilled by the eldest of the clan
Held sacred, trusted, and cared for...
Things like God and family, livestock and land.
Now the truth comes clear and simple
Looking out through the glare of that dirty windshield.
Time and age march onward–
Ever forward, never to retreat nor yield.
Hours and days forge into years
And pass so swiftly from cradle to the grave.
A truth lost on youthful swagger
When you're mounted on a fast horse feeling brave
Yeah, he's halfway down life's trail now
But he doesn't dwell on thoughts of being done.
The way he's got it figured
Life's best blessings and sweetest rewards are yet to come.

The Silent Storyteller

"Daddy, can you come and help me with my spurs?"
Was the pleading question from my teenage son.
So I went over and met him at the kitchen table
Not long after we'd left it when supper was done.
As he and I sat there swapping out the leathers
Going about changing the old for new
I couldn't help but pause to look back upon
All the things that worn old table had been through.

It had arrived from a trip cross-country
After we found it traveling through Taos.
Heavy and rustic with hand-carved sunbursts on the legs
It's a weathered golden brown that's just right in our house.
From holding typical daily meals for us
To being a workbench and taking some abuse
The top's garnered plenty of scuffs and scratches…
Like any family's table, it's seen some varied use.

But particular to our little home
Are the marks and nicks that I love best
The many memories and uses all our own
That serve to distinguish our table from all the rest.
On the surface, you can trace our family's years
In the numbers and letters, stains, shapes and lines
Left when small hands pressed pencil hard onto paper
And beneath it etched into that soft yellow pine.

There's samples of their blocky, early scribble
As well as refined letters in cursive and print;
Subtle, hard-to-see reminders of homework
that provide evidence of all those hours spent.
And yet some result from my own artwork,
From pencil sketches to canvases with oil paint…
Fingertips feel them and a sharp eye spots them
Whether they're deeply embossed or somewhat faint.

On holidays it's held colored eggs or pumpkins,
And at Christmastime it's where all the cookies are made.
It's not only the spot for laying out fine china,
But also where guns are cleaned or card games are played.
Our kids have huddled over it for countless hours
Learning to tie knots or how to plait ropes and strings.
And from time to time it just sits there covered up,
full of mail, documents, car keys, junk and other things.

That table's been home to planning and negotiation -
Where family goals are cooked up along with the meals
And it's a conference place now and then
When Farm Service or NRCS come review our deals.
Some nights I've sat there for hours with furrowed brow,
Pondering and sorting out just how to make ends meet,
While others I might just sit alone with the Good Book
Reminded of the Almighty's promises so complete.

Through busy days and the short hours we sleep it's there,
Ever-present for our joy and pain... laughter and tears
That table's always waiting, as a faithful servant waits
Bearing witness to all our ambitions, hopes and fears...
Centered in our home, sturdy, solid and true,
A constant observer that never speaks a word.
We treasure it as we do an old trusted friend...
The silent storyteller that only a few have heard.

Ranch Wives & the Mama Instinct

From Biblical accounts to classical literature, the love and devotion of mothers has been well documented throughout the ages. However, ranch moms are like no other based on the not-so-common experiences they will inevitably encounter. Some are yoked to the lifestyle by birthright while there are those less fortunate souls who unwittingly marry into it rather blindly. The claim could even be made that these ladies are duped into the plight due to a lack of full disclosure by their prospective ranching mate. I find that explanation a bit too harsh, and instead would say that the young ladies' vision is simply obscured by the romantic visions of ranch life rooted in their subconscious mind after having been planted there by Hollywood movies and childhood stories of chivalrous gentlemen on noble steeds. Actually, they got the chivalrous part right, but that's for another topic in the coming weeks...

My lovely and ever-so-tolerant wife falls into this latter category. She could have done so much better for herself–a predictable home life and husband, quick access to grocery stores, and shopping downtown. But fortunately for me, God had other plans awaiting us. Now mind you, Sam wasn't a city girl completely uninitiated with rural living (and boy, do I feel sorry for those women who come into ranching completely out of their element and no frame of reference for it); her family had been in the dairy business so technically she had a slim advantage over most females marrying into the ranching business... the cows may not have had the same coloring or temperament, but she had at least experienced them.

Ranch moms witness and tolerate more chaos, bedlam and near-delusional thinking in one week than the chief psychiatrist at your local nut house sees in a year, and they manage to do it all with a smile! Well, the smile is there most of the time. It's a sheer wonder that they don't go insane themselves from the repetition of constantly sweeping up mud and dried, crumbled organic material while incessantly reminding the kids (dad is included at this point based on common characteristics and not age) to please remove all footwear at the door. She hauls the groceries along with feed and hay in her car or SUV and endures endless journeys back and forth to town shuttling kids to and from school, FFA meetings, ball practice, livestock judging, birthday parties, school dances and so on. She washes dresses along with dappled green, manure stained jeans, although not necessarily together, and while washing those jeans she's likely to find freakish little surprises inside pockets like: used ear tags or hairy pieces of ear trimmings and/or the bottom half of a scrotum that were all picked up by curious little fingers when the calves were being earmarked and castrated. Venture into a ranch wife's kitchen and you're very likely to find a 50-pound bag of powdered calf milk replacer on the floor or bottles of colostrum in the freezer for the occasional dobie calf that needs to be bottle fed. She learns to accept late nights and early mornings, high fuel costs and paper-thin budgets.

Above all else, ranch wives develop a heightened mothering instinct, always watching, worrying and waiting with baited breath for the next calamity to occur. In terms of protective instincts, they're kind of like the human equivalent of a Brahma cow–calm, loving, and nurturing until danger threatens or something attempts to put their baby in a tight spot. They're perpetually pulling for the underdog, the downtrodden, the runt of the litter. This past weekend's events serve as a perfect illustration of those mama instincts and plain old ranch life peculiarities.

Over this past weekend, our daughter Jacqueline's purebred Brahman cow "Sally" calved with a new little bull calf. With a crossbred or commercial cattle operation like ours, having detailed records of calf birth weights, weaning weights and so on, isn't terribly important. But, for purposes of registering purebred cattle those records are of critical importance and as such, I needed to catch the calf out here in the pasture surrounding the house. From her earliest age when we attempted to halter break her for the show ring, Sally has been ill-tempered and contrary with nearly everyone, but men in particular. With that knowledge and based on my prior experiences with weighing her other calf, I knew that this would be no easy task.

To add an additional wrinkle in my plans, I had managed to jam a cabbage tree palm frond into my left eye the day before and having been to the local eye care center, my vision was blurred from the inflammation in my eye. Nonetheless, the job needed to be done so my son, Jared, and I set out in the truck with a bucket of feed to coax the mad mama cow close enough that we could catch the calf. With my first attempt, I got the calves' left hind leg and was trying my best to drag him back to the truck without getting mauled by Sally. As she continued her frenzied protective efforts by running at me with head lowered eyes bugged out, teats squirting milk below while her bellowing calls rang in my ears, I tried to keep her at bay by placing my free hand on her forehead.

When Jared was younger and would ride his bike around the pasture, Sally would often bluff him and make a half-hearted snorting run at him as he came by. Clearly, Jared still harbored those memories as he sat in the truck watching me attempt to make it back there where I had left the weighing scale and the security of a safety buffer within which to work. Thinking on the fly, I made the decision that I could move more quickly if I picked the calf up which I did while still back peddling. A bad decision, indeed… Sally immediately tried to climb into my arms as well, bawling loudly as she piled into me and knocked me over backwards in a heap. My body stiffened in defensive anticipation of the jarring blows and stomping feet I just knew were going to hit me at any minute, but instead I looked up to see Sally and the calf scampering off in the opposite direction. I scrambled to my feet and jumped back into the truck asking Jared what had happened to him being my backup. He gave me no reply except more bug-eyes and a blank stare.

Waiting for a slight separation between Sally and the calf as they ran down the fence line, I nosed my truck in between and tossed my door open hoping to stop the calf. However, he made it between my door and the fence forcing me to give chase on foot away from the truck yet again. I didn't repeat my mistake this time and kept the calf between me and his mama until I could make it to the tailgate of the truck where I climbed in and then lifted the calf into the bed with me. Just before I yanked the tailgate closed, Sally seemed like she might jump into the back with us but then turned away. She continued running tight laps around the truck as I weighed the bull calf before dropping the gate back down to gently slide him to the ground. Jared got behind the steering wheel and drove us away from them so that we could all four gather our composure and settle down.

I knew that Sam was picking Jacqueline up from softball practice and that they would want to know the calf's weight so I fired off a quick text message mentioning the outcome, my near-mauling from the cow, and how I escaped her by lifting the calf into the back of my truck by his hind legs. Did I get a text message back with something along the lines of a rhetorical "Oh my, are you okay?" Oh, but of course not… Sam's reply to me was simply "Is he ok?" After 18 years of marriage, I should have expected that response, but admittedly it caught me by surprise. What else could I do? I laughed it off and sent her a sarcastic reply back mentioning my own welfare versus that of the calf.

And right there with that one little scenario, the heightened "mama instinct" of both a ranch wife and a mama cow is underscored to perfection as I got it from two directions that afternoon. Was there a second thought for potential injuries to me? Of course not, because I'm not the baby or the underdog! Take it from me fellas, you could walk in the house with your left ear half torn off and dangling by a sliver of the lobe, a muddy hoof print tattooed across your right cheek, and your pant legs shredded like a grass hula skirt appearing as if you'd just finished the championship match of a rugby game and you'd still hear your wife ask that inevitable question: Is the cow/horse (insert your animal or inanimate object of choice here) okay? And, as if to add insult to injury, they always assume that you did something to draw the ire of said animal thereby "asking for it" in the first place.

Men, don't look for any sympathy around the ranch because you're on your own. I think I've finally figured it out though… That overdrive mama instinct is just another of the many tools at their disposal used to get even with us for our lack of full disclosure about all the little unknowns to which they were saddling themselves at the time they uttered the words "I do."

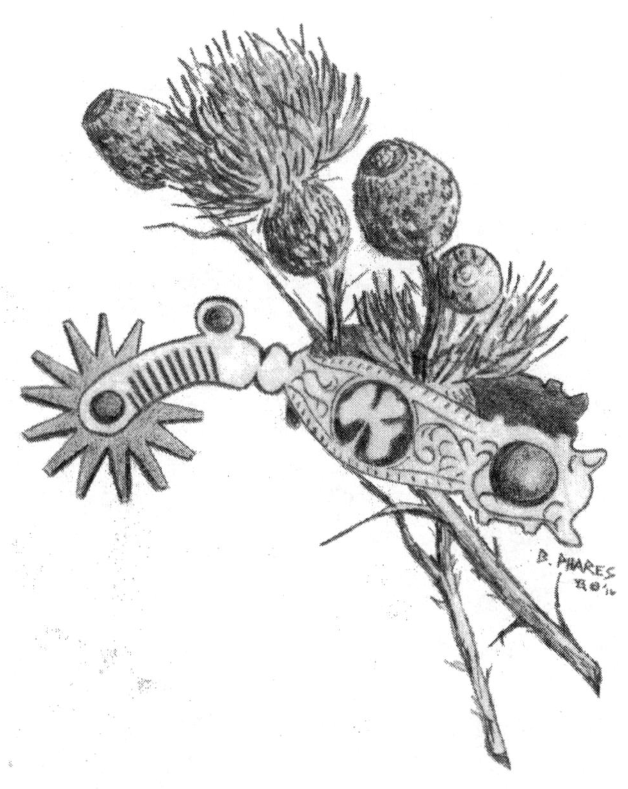

We Buried Mama's Horse Today

We Buried Mama's Horse today
Out between the old barn and the pens…
She rested quiet in the grass almost knowing
That like this day, her time was coming to its end.
My mind trailed back through the years
As we all sat there waiting on the vet to show.
I recalled how Daddy surprised my Mama,
When he got the mare about eighteen years ago.

Mama's first horse had been palomino
So he thought what might be her last horse should be too...
Robin was bright yellow with a big blaze face,
Highlighted by eyes that were sparkling icy blue.
She was a show-stopper at local parades
When all the townsfolk came out to line along the street.
But more than just a piece of equine eye candy;
Ol' Robin turned out to be a horse smart and complete.

Mama rode her when we'd gather cattle
With grandkids piled behind the saddle riding double
Or my brothers might ride her to work
When their horses were lame or had some kinda trouble
Our young ones just learning to ride
Could get on her and she'd plod along plumb lazy
But then again she could get real athletic
While carrying good cow hands 'round cattle acting crazy

The amber rays of the late-day sun shone down
As I watched my daughter lying next to Robin there
While the grass danced gently around them
Swaying softly to the rhythm of late October air
Memories both long forgotten and some brand new
came raining down and flooded through my head…
Ones like the day my young son rode Robin
And had a freak accident that could've left him dead.

Running to turn a yearling back to the herd
Robin jumped when it hit the fence, and Jared fell…
Barbed wire between us, I saw his foot hung stirrup bound
And for a moment I was trapped in a living Hell…
But when he landed that yellow mare pulled up short,
Slid to a stop, dropped her head and stood right there
While the yearling high-tailed it on down the lane
And I sent a prayer of thanks heavenward into the air.

Then there was the day at Buck Island
When she and I kicked up a nest of wild bees
She flew into fits of bucking and kicking
As we hopped and darted amongst the trees.
I could see the big horse wreck coming quick
With water in a ditch to my left and a fence to my right
So I quit the saddle with reins in hand
Landed and kept running till no bees were in sight.

At the time, we had no way of knowing
That Robin wasn't anywhere near feeling her best
Other than a little heavier breathing,
She never quit me when I put her to the test.
But that trip to work wound up being her last one
My saddle would be the last one thrown over her back
She and I had chased her last bunch of cattle
Before returning back home to quietly hang up her tack.

In weeks that followed, I'd seen her weight drop
and her ability to breathe was more difficult yet…
It became clear something just wasn't right
So I placed a call to mama and then one to the vet.
He arrived and carefully looked her over
Then broke the bad news after a deliberate pause.
Her condition and comfort would only worsen…
Some sort of cardio-pulmonary disease was the cause.

With the sun nearly gone from view,
Somber evening shadows stretched out deep and long.
Everything seemed hushed and quiet,
But for a choir of meadowlarks whistling a farewell song.
And all of us stood by quiet and solemn,
As the vet helped ease Robin softly to her end.
We buried mama's horse today
Out between the old barn and the pens.

A Ranch Wife's Bargain

She never bargained for fence staples on the vanity
or cow shit on the floor,
Colostrum* in the freezer, milk replacer in the house
or penicillin in the fridge door.

She never dreamed of being outside in her PJ's
Shivering, pointing a flashlight,
To help him see enough to fix the fence someone hit
Sometime just before midnight.

She never bargained for calls at random hours
About cattle on the road,
Though she's given thought to videoing those trips
For reality TV episodes.

She never expected some of the surprises
She finds when washing clothes…
What makes a boy stuff calf scrotum sacks* in his pockets
She won't even pretend to know.

And, clearly she never bargained for their contents
To be supper on the table!
But when it comes to changes and making adjustments,
She proved she's more than capable.

She never envisioned making trips to the store
Would be a major ordeal,
'Cause she didn't know that home would be so far from town
When negotiating their deal.

She loves their life, their kids and her cowboy
And all that's under his hat,
And though she never bargained for all the cow nonsense,
She's learned to love even that.

* *Colostrum*: the earliest form of milk produced by mammals during late pregnancy that is loaded with natural antibodies and immunoglobulins. Ranchers will often keep some on hand for raising orphaned calves.

* *Calf scrotum sacks*: during castration of bull calves, the lower third to half of the scrotum sack is cut off to expose the testes for removal and young kids are fascinated by the very soft, velvet-like feel of them. When the sacks are cut and thrown in the dirt, kids try to round a few up thinking they're going to salt cure/tan them into some kind of leather goods...parents humor them briefly but making plans for tossing them later.

Almost a Courtroom Cowboy

While it's nothing terribly new,
Knowing lots of other folks do it, too,
I reflect on my life now and again
Considering my choices and where I've been.
I tally all the dues I've paid,
And wonder whether there's any I might trade.

My youth was spent playing and working outside
Around orange groves and prairies wide
Running and riding through grass and trees
Where a boy's mind could drift as it pleased.
Without a doubt I loved the land,
And learned to depict it with my hands.

Little things unseen by most people caught my eye
Like the way sunlight dances on a horse's hide.
From crayons to pencils on to brushes and paint,
I'd set out to draw and show what others can't.
And I didn't stop at what I could paint or draw,
I learned to paint with words conveying what I saw.

Most folks said ranching wouldn't take me too far;
Go to college, be a doc or pass the Florida bar.
So I went and tried the suit and tie…
Stuck in an office just waiting to die
A caged bird just longing to fly.
While the world and time were passing me by…

Sure, I could do the job and do it good,
But just 'cause you can, don't always mean you should.
I'm sure lots of people thought me crazy,
While others probably just thought me lazy…
When I walked out on a legal career
Backtrailing to all that I hold dear.

Family time, livestock and open spaces,
Outweigh courtrooms, big cars, and rat races.
True enough that choice comes with sacrifice
But whether some think it my virtue or vice,
I'm willing to shoulder some early pain
When I can see a bigger long term gain.

Choices saddle us to our path in life
With each one bringing its share of strife,
But in the end there's no reason to complain
Because there's not much that I'd ever change
I'm doing the ranch work I was born into…
While painting and writing about it, too.

Chapter 4

Contemporary Cowhuntin'

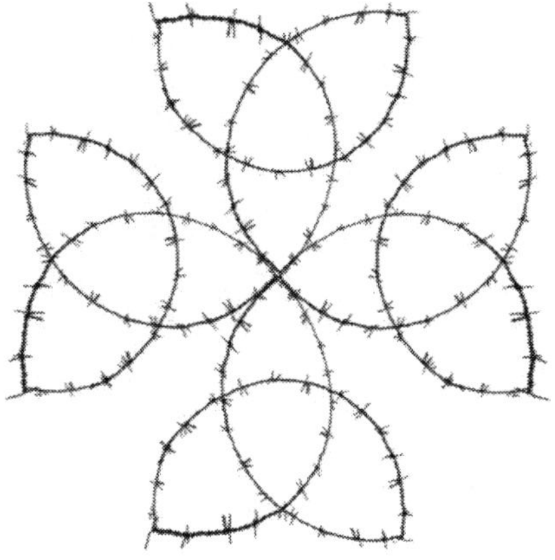

Morning Glory: The Early Start of a Day Working Cows

Though the days of staying out on open range working cattle for weeks on end have long since passed, much of the work remains the same and the days simply start a little bit differently. Instead of arising from a bedroll laid out on the ground in the elements, contemporary cowhunting starts at home and oftentimes goes a little something like this…

All is still and quiet in the last hours of darkness that make up those unique hours of the morning known best by those who either perform shift work or those who find themselves bound to a life in agriculture, whether by birth or choice. The morning coffee is started and soon enough that rich, comforting aroma fills the room. Nobody else has been rousted from their dreams and there's a solace found in the silence. A pleasurable silence because it is fleeting and soon enough will be broken by all the sounds of the day, remaining elusive until the late night hours roll around again and beds are filled once more. About the time the coffee in the cup reaches the point where most folks would philosophically ponder its state of being either half-full or half-empty, it serves as a reminder that everyone else needs to be up and getting ready for the day's work ahead. The shuffle of dresser drawers along with the jingling of spur rowels on worn boots echoes through the rooms before disappearing with the bodies wearing them as everyone heads on outside to the barn.

With a sound somewhere between a creak and a groan, the barn door swings open and a bucket rattles with the sound of feed bouncing off the bottom or sides as it cascades down from the feed scoop above. Stepping back out of the barn, a cadence of short, shrill whistles accompanied by a thorough shaking of that feed bucket in the pre-dawn darkness yields a shadowy string of horses with their hooves falling against the ground behind you as they follow eagerly along. Softly in the distance, Mockingbirds, Cardinals, and a consortium of wading birds all initiate their morning chatter as the stars show their last bit of radiance until nightfall descends upon the landscape once again.

The eastern horizon begins to pick up a rosy-orange glow as clouds begin to take shape, hanging purple and heavy between heaven and earth. During most months in Florida, the warm, damp air carries with it the smell of horse sweat, feed, dirt or mud and composting manure, all mixing together to fill your nostrils with an unmistakable earthy fragrance while you brush down your horse and begin to cinch your saddle on its back. From the very end of November through early to mid-March, a much more comfortable, cooler and drier air settles in for the winter creating a much more pleasant atmosphere for saddling up. Granted, there are those mornings that find anyone yearning for those hazy summer days… Those frigid mornings when the thermometer shows temps hanging in the mid 20's and the once-green Bahia grass is heavy-laden and white with frost because the mercury dipped below 32°F the evening before. For the most part, those winter months aren't so bad though.

Season of the year aside, certain common denominators remain. The cow crew for the day, which most often consists of a mix of family and hired day labor-day workers that make a living hiring out for a day or weeks at a time to ranch families, begin to congregate at the cow pens in those early morning hours. Occasionally, everyone will huddle together around a small fire where a grill holds sausage for breakfast as stories are shared, tall tales are woven and the first pranks of the day are pulled.

After a few final sips from the coffee mugs, everyone unties their reins, steps into a stirrup and drops the opposite leg across the saddle beginning the ride out to meet the day and the first herd of cattle to be gathered. Such is the start of a ranch day filled with cow work. Blessed are they who are fortunate enough to partake of such an experience once, and infinitely blessed are those who do it with regularity, knowing the sense of peace and deep satisfaction that permeates the soul for having lived it.

It's Branding Time Again

Gathering 'round the cow pens, one by one, we've all convened.
It's branding time again for those heifers that were weaned.
We carry in our branding irons... fly dope, ear tags and more...
Propane gas is lit as blowing flames hiss and roar.
Scraps of wood from broken boards are tossed in the branding pot
Just as added measure getting those brands glowing red and hot.

Next we bring the heifers with a holler and a hoot,
Sending them down the alley* towards that humming old squeeze chute.
Its hydraulics go to work and cold steel holds 'em tight...
We give 'em just a minute to get still and quit their fight.
The smell of blood, sweat, and earth rolls up into the air
As hot iron finds its mark burning into bovine hide and hair.

That burning flesh has an odor distinctive and without peers,
And up front by the head-catch, a pocketknife marks their ears.
Next, a new tag is inserted to help ID them on the spot
Before the chute doors fly open and they leave out like a shot.
And the process gets repeated as every heifer is worked through...
Then until next summer rolls around, we bid branding time adieu.

* *Alley*: in a set of pens for working cattle, the alley is a long, narrow passage constructed just wide enough for cattle to pass through it without being able to turn themselves around. In this way, they're forced to continue moving forward until either being "parted" or diverted into another pen somewhere off to one side or the other, or until they reach the end of the alley where there's usually some sort of chute, be it manual or hydraulic to restrain them for vaccinations, deworming treatment, etc.

Caddies, Cattle, And Everything in Between

From those early territorial days right up to the present and for a variety of reasons, people have always been drawn to Florida. In 2015, 1,002 people moved to Florida every single day resulting in 365,702 people per year and an estimated population increase from the current 20.27 million to a projected 26 million plus by the year 2040. Given Florida's surging population and accompanying urban growth, the ranching landscape in the state is an ever-changing one.

With this influx of growth, there's obviously a steady demand for residential development to meet the housing needs of so many families. There is typically a "hold time" between when the developer purchases the land and when they are ready to "turn dirt" or begin construction on the project. Maintaining an agricultural classification on the property for tax purposes within this time frame is essential for the developer to minimize their carrying cost which often results in opportunities for grazing leases.

Some of these grazing leases are typical pasture land and pretty easy to manage while others can offer a multitude of challenges for the cattle owner along with their friends or hired help. Sometimes the challenges come in the form of metal, concrete or other construction materials stored on site that livestock isn't accustomed to being around, sometimes the problems revolve around the fact that multiple people have access to the property and not all of them understand simple ranch rules such as "leave a gate how you found it" resulting in cattle getting out into urban neighborhoods. Still other times the biggest hassles result from the fact that the working facilities and infrastructure employed on leased ground is often less desirable than what is preferable for handling livestock. Since the land isn't owned and the duration of the lease is typically short or uncertain, there isn't much incentive to justify a large investment or capital outlay on building nice cow pens and so forth. As one might imagine, when shortcuts are taken in places like this things can get a little dicey and usually go wrong anytime the need arises to handle or work through the cattle.

A great example of this was a parcel of land that a friend, Steve Jara, leased from Kolter Property Company. While not a full-time rancher, Steve has always been involved in agriculture and built up a small herd of cows that he placed on an undeveloped corner of Kolter's PGA Village bordering Interstate 95 in St. Lucie County, Florida. It seemed like a win-win scenario - Steve got a place to keep his cows and Kolter was able to maintain an agricultural exemption for tax purposes on that piece of land until they were ready to develop it - but boy did we ever get our fair share of headaches out of it.

Every now and then we'd get a call from Steve because one of the Kolter security guards would have called him about a cow running through someone's yard or across one of the fairways on the golf course and we'd have to load up horses, track it down, rope it and pull it on the trailer for a trip back to where it belonged followed by locating the hole in the fence or the open gate left behind by a third-party contractor who was long since gone. Giving chase to cattle around houses, cars, and golf carts on and off of asphalt or concrete mounted on unshod horses is not only difficult but it's not entirely safe either. The lack of traction while trying to run behind a cow to rope it and loose footing to pull it once she's on the end of your lariat can be downright dangerous to the animals and the person riding them. I also remember one Sunday afternoon having to get out on foot in my Sunday-go-to-meeting clothes and chase a calf down alongside the I-95 right of way. I somehow managed to get my hands on him and push him back under the hog wire fence safely away from the traffic going by north and south.

The cow pens we used there were such in name only. Instead of a nice set of wooden pens made from durable cypress, these pens were constructed of wire bull panels nailed up on the posts - functional, but cheap and difficult to use. They didn't have multiple pens to sort and divide the cattle into and there wasn't a central alleyway either, but instead it was one large holding pen with one smaller pen funneling down to a short chute for loading out animals onto trailers. A solid ninety percent of the property was covered in flat woods - native pine and palmetto along with the invasive Brazilian Pepper trees. Much of these woods were so thick as to be nearly impenetrable horseback which made locating and gathering the cattle difficult to say the least. The first few times we tried it and made it to the penning crevice, we'd only get about a third to half of them into the pens while the rest of them jumped like deer, clearing fences and darting off back into those woods.

What followed was a never-ending game of how to build a better mousetrap and what seemed to work best was to bait them into the pens with supplemental feed and hay starting weeks ahead of when Steve planned to work them or sell off calves. Once we'd allowed them enough time to get accustomed to eating inside the crevice area, we'd show up late in the day when it was a near certainty they'd be there eating, just before twilight usually, and we'd sneak up there to quickly close the gate hemming them in for work the following morning. About the time we got fairly proficient with this scheme, everything changed again as Steve was notified that he needed to move the cattle out because Kolter planned to begin another phase of construction on that parcel.

We baited and trapped the first bunch of cows and after that it turned into good old fashioned cow hunting for me, my two brothers, BJ Johnson and Matt Arrieta. The place was covered in standing water and the suffocating summer air hung over us on the day we pulled through the gates to clear the place out. Even in the deep shadows of the pinewoods, there was no relief to be found because it was one of those rare summer days without the presence of an onshore sea breeze from the Atlantic coast. I can feel it even now.

For those uninitiated in the cowboy way, occasions such as this bring out the competitive side of cowboys because contrary to the overly romanticized images most people hold of cowboy life, most of it is very routine and very dirty. So, when opportunities lending themselves to some excitement arise, it invariably evolves into a little friendly competition to see who's going to rope the most cows. That morning the tension was as thick as the summer heat smothering us...

Fanning out in a line across the woods, we sent the dogs out ahead eagerly listening for their barking to echo over the palmettos back to us signaling the location of a cow squatted in hiding deep in the brush. Our wait was not a long one and the explosion of hooves thundering in the muddy ground below and underbrush crashing around us drowned out the steady roar of traffic on the nearby interstate as we raced to converge on all the barking and bellowing. As I mentioned, each of us was looking to outdo the other so not only was it a race to reach the cow before she got into thicker cover, but it was a race to see who was going to tally the first catch of the day. Matt Arrieta has always been one of the handiest dayworkers around and there's not much he loves more than seeing the loop of his lariat settle over the head of a cow in need of catching. He loves it so much in fact, that he's notorious for bumping your horse, doing a little rubbing on the run, or flat out cutting you off once you get a cow lined out ahead of your horse and loop. Needless to say, he made the first catch of the day and then we began the process of navigating out of the woods to the trailer for loading. Of course she pulled back and fought, sail fishing on the end of the lariat line and wrapping around trees the whole way.

The morning continued in similar fashion with prolonged periods of riding and tracking, sweating and searching, sporadically interrupted with a mad dash to rope a cow or yearling. We were lucky enough to chase a few of them out into the open and catch them there where you could easily pull them onto the trailer but most of them were caught in the pinewoods and fought their way to the trailer. By the time we got the last one loaded that day, our horses and dogs were completely spent and we felt pretty drained as well. It was the kind of experience you wouldn't trade for a million dollars but at the same time you wouldn't give a wooden nickel for the chance to do it again.

Be happy while you're living, for you're a long time dead.

- Scottish Proverb

Showers on Sunday

Sunday morning showers
Drifting slowly to the east
Washing down the land
And your soul to start the week
Horses stand with heads bowed down
Echoing their silent "Amens"
As Heaven-sent rain falls down
To wash, to purge, and to cleanse.

Backyard Cattle

If you've never worked backyard cattle,
You've no idea of the treat you're missin'
I'll give you just a taste of it
Should you care to sit and listen...
Whether done by necessity
For tax exemptions and the like
Or based on overzealous notions
About the romantic cowboy life,
City folk will buy a few cows
With no management plan in mind
Then network amongst their friends
Searching for ranchers or experts on bovines.

Once wild and wooly cattle
On pastures with far-flung fence lines,
They're now on little ranchettes
Expected to be urbane and more refined.
When you show up to pen these cows
Events yet to unfold are anybody's guess.
There's barely perimeter fences...
The pens are guaranteed to be a mess.
Boards have fallen on the ground
And gates are hanging by a single hinge
Ain't enough pens to sort 'em out proper;
Their chincy nature just makes you cringe.

Now to get 'em rounded up,
You might dodge goats and a few jackasses, too.
But only after several times
Of them running the herd back on top of you...
Gently you funnel them through,
As the rickety pens shake and sway.
With any kind of luck at all,
The job will get done with none getting away.
I'm proud these folks like cattle
And feel like they're supporting the cowboy way,
But just between you and me...
I'm sure glad I don't have to fool with 'em every day!

Raining Complaints

They say a cowman ought not grumble
About getting hit with too much rain.
Some say it's somewhere just short of sinning
If, on that subject he dares to complain.
People who care for and tend to livestock
Usually end up being resilient and tough...
But after forty rainy days and nights,
Even old man Noah had seen enough!
Your Good Book goes on and spells it out-
In all things 'tis best to moderate...
Just a reminder from me to you, Lord
As I wade to open the gate...

Dayworking Surprises

You never know what surprises lay in store for you when hiring on to daywork at someone else's place, and especially so if it's your first time hiring on with a particular outfit.

Sometimes it's a bad surprise, like showing up to work and finding a cobbled together mess of busted boards and rusty wire they attempt to pass off as cow pens suitable for working their cattle through, or being told not to bring your lunch that they'll provide it for you only to watch the man pull out a loaf of white bread and a single pack of Oscar Mayer bologna. Possibly the worst of surprises is stepping into a set of cow pens, spotting flood lights installed in key positions and realizing you're in for a hell of a long day. Such a setup is a sure sign that you're working for the miserly sort who figures that since they've got you for day wages it's to their benefit to squeeze every hour out of you they can get; a practice generally viewed as a faux pas in the day working community. Other times it might be a good surprise like when the rancher you're working for lays out a big spread for lunch, gives you plenty of extra time after lunch allowing for a good nap, or any number of other pleasantly unexpected things.

And of course, you encounter those surprises now and then that end up being a comedic spectacle. I can recall two occasions where I was dealt such surprises and while they were years apart both of them involved donkeys.

The first donkey episode took place when my youngest brother, Brent, along with Frank Lewis asked me to help them work cows for Mrs. Syfrett at her place in Basinger. It was an early summer morning with the dew still lingering on the grass and the last remnants of fog dissipating as we rode off from the pens to gather the cattle. It was the kind of morning where everything seems too good to be true-and indeed it was. We hadn't made it more than a quarter mile from the trailers when we rode up on a pair of donkeys standing together in the pasture, which isn't as uncommon as it first may sound because any more people keep the donkeys around to fend off the coyotes that have grown to become such a big problem in Florida. Considering I was riding a green broke horse, I was really keyed into her every move not knowing how she'd respond to the donkeys. To my surprise, she walked right by them seemingly paying them little to no mind.

We made it just far enough past them that I had breathed a sigh of relief and relaxed ever so slightly in the saddle when out of the blue she dropped her head and broke into crow-hopping around in a half circle to the right. I stuck to her for the first few hops until she came back to the ground one time and sucked back under me going to the left all at once. Forward momentum kept me moving to the right and I was shot from the saddle like an oversized lawn dart while everyone doubled over in their saddles with laughter at my expense. Thankfully, the only wound I had was my bruised pride after letting that little filly catch me by surprise and get the best of me. She had never even offered to buck prior to that - not even when I started her under saddle - and she never gave me another minute's worth of trouble afterwards, but there sure must've been something she didn't like about that jack and jenny pair on that particular morning.

Roughly a decade would pass before my next dayworking adventure with donkeys, and it proved even more interesting. A friend of mine had asked me to get together a small crew to work his cows explaining that they were pretty easy to gather and handle. So, not knowing much more than that, I recruited Hobert Lee as well as BJ Johnson, who had been dayworking for us at our ranch for years, and we showed up right after daylight one morning to get the job done. Once again we learned that there were some donkeys-the miniature variety at that-on the property. We were told that the little jack was pretty much a pet and would be wearing a blue halter but it was suggested that we ought to be careful to watch our dogs because he was pretty territorial and protective of both the jennies and the cows so as such he'd probably try to bite and stomp our dogs.

We struck out riding our horses down the main grade that ran the length of the ranch engaging ourselves in the customary morning chatter that most town folk typically banter about in a coffee shop-the weather, politics, the latest rumors, and so forth. The country was open and scarce of trees save for just a few oak and cabbage tree hammocks along with even fewer scattered pines, so there wasn't much cow hunting to be done but rather just ride straight to them, get 'em bunched up, let the dogs circle around them a few times to settle them down and then drive 'em on back to the pens. Everything seemed simple enough up to that point, but as we drew closer to the cows that's when things went from mundane to nearly insane.

The mini donkeys were off to our right with that little jackass positioned between the cows and the group of jennies who were by now twitching their ears and focused on what we might be doing. Likewise, the cows had also spotted us and with heads held high began spinning around in small circles looking back over their shoulders and thinking about which way they wanted to break and run. As the dogs trotted just out ahead of our horses, we were just before whistling them into action with the cue to go hold up the cows when the little jack broke into a dead run heading towards us, but more specifically towards the dogs.

The little jack had his ears pinned back with his head dropped low as he closed in on the dogs, and I'm sure he was used to coyotes and other dogs tucking tail and running in the opposite direction as fast as possible but such was not to be the case that day. Both my dog Cotton and BJ's dog went on the offensive meeting the little jack before he ever made it near us and I'm not sure who was the most surprised by the unexpected turn of events - me and BJ or the jackass. He tried his usual repertoire of tricks pawing with his front hooves, kicking with the back, and trying to bite the dogs before realizing that they weren't having any part of it. It was almost like the cartoons you see as a kid when the light bulb appears over a character's head because you could almost see the little jack's expression change as a look of panic came into his eyes. Cutting a wide arcing circle, he tried to distance himself the dogs but they were locked on him like heat seeking missiles such that no matter which way he turned or much he zig-zagged he couldn't shake them.

All the while, we're yelling, hollering, and popping our whips at the dogs, "get out… leave 'em alone… get outta there damn it!" It was all wasted air. They were green-eyed monsters at that point with only one goal and that was to get ahold of that jackass. Like kicking over a bucket of roaches, cows scattered in nine directions amidst the ruckus of cracking cow whips, cussing, shouting, barking, and braying that rose like a cloud over the pasture. BJ's dog caught one of those long, slender ears and sat back on it as my dog reached out and clamped down squarely on the jack's muzzle and upper lip. Both dogs sat down and anchored the jackass right where they stood. About the time we tried to get down from the horses to go get them off, the jack found the energy to try making another escape and bolted ahead into a small cluster of brush.

BJ and I both jumped from our horses and followed them into the canopy. The little jackass was braying and squealing for all he was worth with my dog still on his lip and BJ's dangling like an oversized earring when we reached them. BJ was ahead of me and grabbed the jack's halter as I flailed a tie rope at the dogs to get them off. After a few times of the dogs trying to sneak back up there to get another bite, they finally gave it up and stayed back out of the way. Fortunately for us and for him, there weren't any major cuts or tears but rather several puncture wounds. We knew that if we turned the jack loose the circus act would be back underway, so we decided to tie him to a nearby tree by his halter and come back to turn him loose once we had the cows penned.

After letting the dogs cool down in a ditch, we managed to get the cows bunched back together and drove them on up to the pens, got our work done and then went back to turn the jackass lose once our horses and dogs were loaded on the trailer. We went back there to work cows several more times but that little mini jackass always steered well clear of us after that first day. I guess you'd say he wasn't too fond of surprises either.

"A raggy colt often made a powerful horse."
~ Irish Gaelic Saying

From Mud to Dust

From mud to dust and back again.
It's one or the other in the pens.
Settled or splattered here and there
It's on the boards or in the air.

Rest assured the change comes fast
Today's dust was mud day before last
And don't matter which form it comes in
It'll be up your nose and on your chin

A blend of earth and rain so pure
Pounded by hooves and mixed with manure,
Wet sometimes then dry again
Covering you and all your friends

Cowboys and cattle are here then die
But mud and dust remain beneath the sky
Through all the summers and all the frosts
The ground holds secrets of days we've lost

In all the years it never changes,
Instead it simply rearranges...
Tried and true, the cycle never ends
From mud to dust and back again.

View From the Saddle

Some men like the view from inside a penthouse suite
Others prefer the chaos found on crowded city streets.
Some guys prefer looking out from atop the mountain's peak
Or peering over sparkling water at beaches, lakes or creeks.
And some figure there's no better way to spend the day
than chasing a dimpled ball down an open fairway.

Some fellas take delight in cars and tinkering under the hood;
To them there ain't nothing better than fast ones looking good.
Some guys, from fans to amateur or professional athletes,
live for the view at stadiums and fields where they compete.
Still others find nothing better than eyeballing pages in a book,
Or fresh foods and shiny metal pans in kitchens where they cook.

I've seen all that and more throughout my years
And some delighted me while others pained me to tears…
But a truth I've learned through lessons both good and bad:
People ain't all made the same…a fact of which I'm glad.
'Cause if we were all alike, life would surely be a bore,
Always doing the same thing and doing it again once more.

Peace for me is atop a horse looking far as I can see
Under the sun, two working as one, moving swift and free
No matter whether in summer heat or winter cold,
That weightless feeling of freedom never grows old.
It liberates my soul and unleashes my mind to roam…
Sitting in the saddle is right where I'm most at home.

Beefsteak and Bourbon

Perched upon my saddle yesterday,
Aimlessly, a thought occurred to me:
There's lots of things in this old world
That fit together so perfectly.
For instance, coffee and cold weather
or salt and butter for your grits.
And bacon goes just right with eggs
like cane syrup poured on hot biscuits.

Many are simple and southern
Like brown gravy over white rice,
Peanut butter and bananas,
Or some sweet tea poured over ice.
There's Saturdays and college football
Followed by Sunday morning preachin'
Hot summer days and ice cold beer,
Shorts, bikinis and sunny beachin'.

Then you've also got famous pairs
Like Bob Wills and Texas Swing.
Slide a little further to the east
For those delta blues and BB King.
There's Hemingway and his great novels
Or Kris Kristofferson's well-penned songs.
While old Missouri gave the U.S.
Frank and Jesse - both long since gone.

We could run on near forever
Building a never-ending list.
Everyone's got their favorites;
Surely by now, you've got the gist.
But since it's drawing close to supper
My mind's on burgers and beer from Shiner*
Or beefsteak and single barrel bourbon...
For me there's simply nothing finer!

* *Shiner*: Shiner, Texas is home to Spoetzel Brewery which has produced fine craft beers for more than 100 years now.

Ranchers: Masochists or Just Plain Nuts?

Have you ever wondered just why you do some of the things you do, especially when it's an activity or decision that always seems to be counterproductive? Every person is guilty of having some little tick, habit or quirky attribute that they either unknowingly exhibit or they do know that it's there and they simply choose to ignore it. Sometimes, a large group of people can all share a common counterproductive behavior...which brings us to ranchers.

Ranchers fall into that second category–we know we're engaged in an activity that causes continual aggravation but we're seemingly gluttons for punishment and keep going back for more. As a matter of fact, if cattle people were featured on Fox News Channel's light-hearted segment "Normal or Nuts," Dr. Keith Ablow would likely turn in his psychiatric license rather than attempt to explain a rancher's rationale for putting up with cattle. What other group of people would so willingly devote themselves to something that is such a mix of pleasure and raw, unnerving irritation?

No matter how well your cattle handle, no matter how much training you think you've done to insure that they behave well, their stubborn streak will ultimately reveal itself. In efforts to elude capture they'll squat and hide under trees or jump in the nearest ditch or pond until forced to move somewhere else. You can gather them on horseback and think you've got them licked with everything rolling along slick as a whistle until, at that moment when you least expect it, one of them will raise their head and tail before bolting from the bunch inciting others to freely participate in their rebellion. And when you and/or several dogs persuade them rejoin the herd, they haven't learned any lesson; you've not dissuaded them one bit because the same cow will try it again and again until they're confined within the cow pens.

Dealing with cattle was succinctly and accurately described by the fictional character Wil Anderson (played by John Wayne) in the movie,

The Cowboys when he says, "You know, trail driving is not Sunday School picnic. You got to figure you're dealing with the dumbest, orneriest critter on God's green earth. The cow is nothing but trouble tied up in a leather bag–and the horse ain't much better."

And once you've gotten them corralled in the pens, the fun doesn't stop. Some of them stubbornly ring and twist while others prefer to drop their heads and make a run at you with slobber and snot flying sideways as green material that used to be grass goes shooting out the back end in a shotgun pattern showering down anything nearby. Working cattle for just one day can set family to feuding in an endless session of bickering and make spouses yearn for divorce.

Even still, we've yet to discuss the sheer delight of being awakened out of peaceful slumber by the 2am phone call from the county dispatcher at the sheriff's office alerting you to the fact that a vehicle left the highway and took out several hundred yards of your fence causing curious cows to stream forth from their normal abode. Or she could simply be calling to inform you that the Harry Houdini of cows has managed to find it's way onto the road for a midnight stroll without breaking a single strand of barbed wire in the endeavor. Either way, nothing compares to the soft glow of bovines under flashing blue lights as you and law enforcement escort them back home. The real irony brought to light is that you realize cows feign stupidity because here, in the dark of night with some gentle coaxing, they can run straight back to the exact spot where they made their exodus from the pasture yet they can't manage to find a wide open gate when you're horseback and trying to move them during daylight hours.

So we're back to the inexplicable question of why we keep raising cows. Maybe it's simply bred into us or is a product of our upbringing– we do it because "daddy did it". A friend once told me that vegetable farming was an addiction, and like any drug addict that goes unchecked, farmers would sell off a little piece of land here and there to keep feeding their farming habit. Perhaps there's an aspect of addiction to ranching as well.

More than likely, we do it because all those irritations and eccentricities of the cow seem to fade from memory as we take pride in knowing that we're feeding our great nation, along with many other nations, as we gaze across the pastures and woodlands that make up our ranch lands. Add we take pleasure too in the sense of contentment within the soul that results from seeing cattle scattered across the landscape with calves nursing at their side. Suddenly, the answer to our lingering question becomes abundantly clear and logical. We keep doing it because the rewards outweigh the accompanying vexations and tribulations of owning cattle. Ranchers do what they do because deep down inside they love it and they get to experience extraordinary things in an otherwise ordinary life.

"The grace of God is found between the saddle and the ground."

~ Irish Proverb

Cold March Wind

It's a cold March wind
That finds us working again,
Pushin' horns and leather
While cussin' this foul weather.
December through March passed
Without frost laid on the grass.
Trees have all now bloomed out green,
Coats be damned... it's time for Spring!
But Jack Frost gets one last chance,
Late or not, he's still gonna dance.
So we tolerate morning's chill
As we practice our cowhand skills...
Well-knowing that sooner than not,
Summer days will be too damn hot!

Brushin' the Gray Mare

I'm out here at the barn in waning afternoon light
Tending to my chores before day gives way to night.
There's just a hint of coolness left hanging in the air
And, with springtime near the weather's looking pretty fair.
The horses and that dobie calf* all seem content and happy,
But their shedding winter coats got 'em looking awful shabby.

The gray mare stands there quiet just nibbling at her oats
With matted hair a sign that she's shedding her winter coat.
She's got a haggard, worn appearance of ten years plus,
But she's really much younger... a diamond in the rough.
Opening the gate brush in hand, she gives me just a glance
With each and every stroke, her beauty is enhanced.

Floating softly to the floor of mingled dirt and hay
Hundreds of hairs drift down like a fine and misty rain.
They lie there glittering as if gold dust in a creek,
As between the boards and crevices, fading sunlight streaks.
I brush her from top to bottom as well as front to rear...
The peaceful sounds of her chewing echoing in my ears.

Her hair needs plenty more work, but for today I'm through.
She'll be shed out slick and shiny in just a week or two.
Then pleasant springtime months will pass to hot summer days...
While I go about my work, the mare will stand out back and graze.
With smooth short hair and green grass, she'll shimmer in the sun,
And seeing her there I can be proud of a job well done.

* Dobie calf: a variation of "dogie," used to describe an orphaned, or motherless calf.

Learning How To Leg 'Em

Return now down your life's path,
To your first time working a calf.
Such fun you had way back then
Sitting by that crowding pen.
Most calves would wad up tight to hide
But a few ran bouncing off the sides.
Then the cowboys would gather 'round
Flipping those calves upon the ground.
Vaccinate...deworm...castrate
When all done they're out the gate.

One day you find it's now your turn
And you're young...eager to learn.
Far from reaching your teenage years,
You try hard to hide all signs of fear.
Having seen the best of examples,
Your cowhand training's been quite ample.
It's the right hind leg you're seekin'
When behind the calf you come a sneakin'.
And one last important little trick...
Don't touch their rump or else they'll kick!

You're set and ready to take a stab...
As nervously you reach and make your grab.
Leg in hand, you hold on so tight,
As the calf jerks with all its might!
Arms shaking you turn and shift,
Until that foreleg starts to lift.
Now you drop and lean back taut
While giving meds, the other fellas squat.
Once done with a calf that's stout,
You climb on top and ride him out!

Give back to nature, what nature has given to you.

- Gaelic Proverb

Fifty-five and Falling: The Wet Winter Blues

It's fifty-five and falling,
Both the temperature and the rain.
Most folks don't like it wet and cold
And I shouldn't much complain,
Because all that fussin' and griping
Ain't ever made the weather change.

I drift on back to the barn
While watching the cattle graze,
And ragged clouds slide southeast
In winter twilight's purple haze…
It's another front sweeping down the state
And heading towards the Florida Straits.

It's 55 and falling,
A drab and dreary gray.
Water table's above the ground
And we get more rain every day.
Soggy boots…and wet leather…
And muddy clothes are here to stay.

Standing under the old barn
With raindrops running off the roof,
It's nice to be under cover,
Somewhere dry and waterproof.
As I pull the saddle from my partner,
And he shifts his weight to one hind hoof.

It's fifty-five and falling,
Sure to be colder by daylight.
Departing clouds reveal the stars
Foretelling a clear and chilly night.
But right now I'll go sit by the fireplace
With its blue smoke chasing the moonlight…

Yessir, it's fifty-five and falling,
And everything's alright.

Rowdy Nights and Rough Days

I got the idea for this piece of poetry while we were working our cows one day when BJ Johnson reminded us all of a story that happened quite a few years back when one of the younger guys dayworking for us "tied one on" the night before he came to work… A time before we used the hydraulic squeeze chute to catch the calves for castrating, dehorning and vaccinating; a time when the older generation took great joy in letting the calves get on up there in age and weight before making all of us jump in the crowding pen to catch them, throw them down and do all the work right there like they had always done it. Manhandling 450 pound and heavier yearling calves was tough, gritty but fun in every way for young men who wanted to prove their worth!

You could hear that old Gooseneck rattle,
And see the dust trail when he cleared the gate.
His horse was wide-eyed and just a-shakin',
As he skidded up next to us running late.
A bit of steam rolled from beneath his hood
As he spilled outta the dented pickup door.
With a half-cocked grin he winked at us,
His shirt half-untucked showing off his drawers.
Then with Herculean effort,
He reached up and swung into the saddle
Where he settled like a limp dishrag
Making us wonder if he'd even stay a-straddle.

Lord knows where he'd been last night,
Or if he'd even bothered going to bed.
His breath of booze could turn the sober drunk;
While a black hat framed blue eyes turned slightly red.
We gathered in the first bunch of cattle
And set about working them through the pens.
When it came time to leg and throw those yearlings
That bourbon went to sweating out through his skin.
The aroma swirled around us thick-like
Such that it nearly choked us to our knees.
"You ought not go chasin' dry cows on week nights,"
We chided as we started to poke and tease.

Those yearlings were downright ornery
With lots of kickin', snortin' and hookin'.
The kid was turning fifty shades of green
But that's the price ya pay for stayin' out jukin'.
Like a good sport, he took his medicine
And did so without uttering a word of fuss.
He sucked it up and stayed 'til the job was done
Though we thought for sure he'd fall out on us.
We've all raised a little cane now and then,
And to be totally honest, some still do.
But without doubt, trouble's sure to come courting,
When you drain the bottle instead of a glass or two.

When A Hard Day's Work Is Done

Whoopin' and ridin' hell-bent for leather...
It was a day full of high tails and floppin' ears,
But ain't been a cow yet these boys can't outrun.
And now we've stripped our saddles; hung up our gear.

As shadows run long and conversation does, too.
We share stories made new and those of old...
Like the one 'bout Matt's rope takin' his thumb;
Still good... no matter how often it gets told.

A fiery sunset fades to purple and pink
While sweat stained horses quietly graze.
It's tailgate sittin' and cold beer sippin'
As we slow it down and call it a day...

Ninety in November

Every day's the same old thing...
Like a scratched and broken record
Just repeating itself over and over
Until you've grown weary and bored.
The same blue skies and sunshine...
The same sweaty, sticky mess...
It's like summer just won't leave us,
Refusing to relinquish or acquiesce.
Most folks would gladly take it
Over huddling near glowing embers,
But not so much here in Florida
When it feels like Ninety in November...

Well, the local weather anchors love it
As do all the snowbirds that came south,
But every day of near record highs
Brings more cussin' from my mouth...
I know folks that ranch out west
Tending their cattle in winter snow,
And I damn sure wouldn't trade places
But what's wrong with 50's for some lows?
That would make things feel just right
For that fire with crackling embers
And we could then forget the days
Of it feeling like ninety in November.

When We're Bringin' In The Bulls

It's December in South Florida
When cattle breeding season starts.
And to see those bulls chasin' after cows,
Sure brings joy to a cowman's heart.
By now, ranchers have culled the ones
Failing the vet's breeding soundness test...
Throughout the Fall, they've hit all the sales,
Seeking replacements they deem the best.
For countless hours they've studied EPD's,
'Til numbers pile up and their brain is full!
Such is the way it goes each year,
When we're bringin' in the bulls.

After a summer spent on feed and grass,
These "dads" have gotten back into shape.
They've pawed the ground and dug deep holes,
Just waitin' on their chance to propagate.
So by starlight's glow we catch our horses,
Brush them down and saddle up just right...
Together then, as family and friends,
We ride to meet morning's first light.
Smiling, laughing and cuttin' the fool,
Most times things go along uneventful.
No matter what, we sure do have fun
When we're bringin' in the bulls!

Caffeine and Kerosene

The west wind howls,
The trees shake and sway…
Just before sunrise
On a cold winter's day.
And glad am I,
Not to be gathering cattle
Freezing my rear end
On a cold leather saddle.

Instead it's comfort in a cup
of dark, rich caffeine
And warmth from Jet A*,
clear, pungent kerosene.
Sweet and strong when first lit
its orange flame fades to blue
And a wave of heat rolls out
Slowly washing over you.

Quiet and coffee
Before anyone's risen;
Some folks won't ever know
The simple pleasure they're missing…
The sunrise glows bright
like this kerosene heater
And the dog curls beside it
While I write in rhyme and meter.

* *Jet A*: fuel used for jets and other aircraft powered by gas-turbine engines. Other than a few additives in modern jet fuel, kerosene and Jet A are nearly identical so can be substituted for one another as a fuel source in heaters.

Chapter 5

Ranching Ain't All Roses and Rainbows

Heavy Weather

The idea for this one–comparing heavy weather and the hidden, everyday burdens people carry inside that weigh them down – came to me after a few days of really wet weather streaming in from the Gulf of Mexico earlier this week.

Heavy weather's brewin' in the sky
And trouble's stirring in my soul;
Feels like my heart's as dark and wild
As those cold, gray clouds that twist and roll.
I can't be sure of what's coming next,
No one ever knows what lies in store…
I'm just tired of hanging onto nothing,
Quietly waiting for something more.

There were many days now long since gone
When I was a high riding hero
But this morning I sit on my horse
Feeling like nothing more than a zero.
Running on eight years plus now,
I've had this run of hard living and tough luck
It's kinda like cinching your saddle each day,
To a horse that never gives up the buck.

Like my persistent hardships and heartaches,
The rain just keeps on coming down.
It pools on horse hide shining
Then runs like little rivers to the ground.
Beneath this sweat-stained hat from Greeley*,
A tattered slicker and old worn-out memories
Remain loosely draped around me
While heavy weather's brewin' on a coastal breeze.

* *Greeley*: a little tip of the hat to my friend, Trent Johnson and his staff at Greeley Hat Works, makers of the finest custom headwear anyone could ask for.

Bitter

This day's been gray and cloudy
An awful lot like my head.
I've been sittin on this porch
Since I first rolled outta bed.
Watching cows all bedded down
With a cold front pushin' through.
It's on somber days like this
My thoughts trail back to you.

It was the winter before last
When you packed your things and left
I'd been out to check the heifers...
Rode back in a victim of theft.
You took my love, and some say my mind
Worst of all, I don't know why...
Lipstick on the bathroom mirror
Said "I love you, but it's good-bye"

Finding your saddle in the barn
And tire tracks spun across the dirt
Just left me more confused
Sinking in a sea of hurt.
Did ya find someone better
Or just miss the glitz of town?
Been twenty-four months now baby
And ain't a soul seen you come 'round.

I hate the days like this one
When I sit here all alone
With silence only broken
By the wind's solitary moan.
Day old coffee's damn sure bitter
Halfway down inside my cup
IOI Proof makes it better
As I turn the bottle up...

When the Wicked Wind Wails

When the wicked wind wails
As the night storms roll...
Fear courses through your veins
And whips at your very soul.

Like a dark horse unseen
Racing shadows of the night,
Stirred in a frenzied panic
It runs hidden outta sight.

Crashing headlong at you
And anything in its way,
Knowing you can't control it
You just hunker down and pray.

Gone... as swiftly as it came.
Now silence the only sound,
And through the ragged clouds
A half-moon peeks at the ground...

Softly shining its light
She seeks to see what remains
Of the broken-hearted souls
Living out here on the plains.

Darker Days

In the darkness before dawn,
I woke up to the sound of rain
Tapping soft upon my window
Stirring thoughts of you inside my brain.
Tangled up in cotton sheets
And your memory again.
I'm a self-convicted prisoner;
everything lost except my pain…

Far off, I hear the highway
Taunting me to chase after you
But instead I simply lay here,
Just me and these Monday morning blues.
How do I move forward…
And what the hell should I do?
I see you in my dreams at night;
The wind whispers your name to me, too.

Outside it's cold and bitter,
The morning sky draped in solid gray
I stumble down the porch steps
Spilling my coffee along the way.
Then I head over to the barn,
Feed the horses to start my day.
I turn your buckskin mare loose
And throw my saddle on the bay.

Some days come down easy
And nearly everything feels alright.
But the ones like today,
Are pure hell for me to face and fight.
Since you left me and this ranch,
There ain't a whole lot that feels right.
I miss your smile by day
And your soft embrace throughout the night.

I've sure enough got my good days,
And those where my back's against the wall.
Yes, some are better than others,
But ones like this are the worst of all,
Painful, sharp reminders
Of last year's early Fall...
When you and your love left me
As weeping angels came to call...

Thirteen Wreaths

This is one of those poems that practically wrote itself while I was driving home to the ranch after attending an event promoted by the organization, Wreaths Across America.

I laid thirteen wreaths by headstones
On the twelfth day of December
For thirteen patriots and heroes
To Honor and remember.

I left the ranch behind me
Not quite sure what lay in store
But I had a calling in my heart
Quite different than any one before
Come Christmastime most folks feel
Much more inclined to freely give
To those less fortunate souls in need,
But what of those who no longer live?

Brave souls who left behind families
That have now gone on up above
After answering the call to service
Enabling us to live the life we love.
What of our brothers and sisters
Who served a grateful nation?
Though they've passed to rest in peace
They are deserving of mindful meditation.

Such were my thoughts and feelings
As I drove along my way
Through backwoods to city cemetery
For Wreaths Across America Day.
Evenly spaced and orderly,
Stars and Stripes lined the driveway in
Leading guests to the ceremony
Attended by strangers, family and friends.

The bugler played *To the Colors,*
And the preacher shared a prayer.
Old Glory popped in the wind;
The scent of pine lingered in the air.
Next came The Pledge and Anthem,
A stirring a cappella version,
Followed by ceremonial wreaths
In an armed forces branch presentation.

Gold Star families shared their stories
Of tragic loss and hope with the crowd
Placing wreaths for their fallen loved ones
As bagpipes echoed a hymn sweet & loud.
Barely had he finished with Amazing Grace
When in salute, the Rifle fired;
Followed by haunting and poignant Taps
And then the colors were retired.

Drifting to the central driveway,
The young and old formed up in lines.
Each person taking their turn
Collecting circular boughs of pine.
Then returning to green hillsides
With reverent heart and wreaths in hand,
I quietly spoke each name aloud…
Grateful for service to God, Country & man.

Whether raising cattle in the country
Or jockeying a desk in town
We're all indebted to our warriors
For the sacrifices they laid down.
As I made it back to the ranch
Dropped off the road and cleared the gate,
I knew that despite all our differences,
Our armed forces unite a nation great.

I laid thirteen wreaths by headstones
On the twelfth day of December
For thirteen patriots and heroes
To honor and remember.

Chapter 6

Catch-As-Catch-Can

Epilogue

Catch-as-catch-can is a phrase that extends back to at least the 14th century and the Oxford English dictionary describes it as expressing "laying hold of in any way, each as he can" or everyone for himself; grab what you can. On the ranch, it's used at times when it doesn't matter how you get your lariat settled onto the bovine target in front of you, no matter whether it's flashy and stylish or fumbling and ugly, you've just got to make sure you get the critter caught. Catch-as-catch-can is all about getting the job done, and for me personally, the phrase is a good way to describe how I utilize my oil paintings, photography and writing to document and share Florida's cow culture with those who aren't fortunate enough to see it firsthand.

Art comes in many forms and among my blessings I count the fact that I'm adept at several of them. At its base level, art is about connections between people, places, and things in spite of the boundaries of place, time, language, or any other limiting factor. For me, visual art like my sketches, paintings, and photography is a universal language that transcends all barriers by laying bare basic truths and speaking to the commonality that all people share.

Having interspersed photos and some of my art sketches alongside various stories and poems throughout the book at junctures where I felt like a particular visual image enhanced the accompanying written word, I thought I'd conclude with a compilation of additional photographs I've had the opportunity to capture (some with a Canon and telephoto lens, others via an iPhone camera in the heat of the moment) while working cattle. My primary aim has always been, and will continue to be, using my art and writing to capture and convey the simple beauty of the everyday sights we see, the sounds echoing in our ears, and the feelings evoked on our Florida ranch lands because the cowhunter culture and landscape are worthy of preserving and perpetuating.

Slàinte Mhrath! (To your good health)

Horses lined up by the cow pens *waiting to work at Lazy JP Ranch near Okeechobee, Glades County, FL*

Brian Phares & Brent Phares take a pause in their work.
Lazy JP Ranch, Okeechobee, FL

Letting the dogs hold up cattle on the open prairie next to Lake Okeechobee. Lazy JP Ranch. Glades County, FL

Cows jockey for position in one of the cow pens at Lazy JP Ranch
Glades County, FL

Horses stand waiting for work on a winter morning.
Lazy JP Ranch, Glades County, FL

Jared Phares looks over some heifers in the crowding pen at Lazy JP Ranch, Okeechobee, FL.

A recently weaned heifer with fresh ear marks and brand.
Lazy JP Ranch, Okeechobee, FL

A calf at Lazy JP Ranch stands in the hopper on a spring morning waiting to receive calf hood vaccinations.

Matt Arrieta sits atop the cow pens at Lazy JP Ranch
Glades County, FL

A large Seminole chickee in the edge of a hammock at the Brighton Reservation, Glades County, FL.

BJ Johnson cracks his cow whip to turn some cattle at Lazy JP Ranch, Okeechobee, FL

Brian Phares sorting through some cattle, Lazy JP Ranch.
Glades County, FL

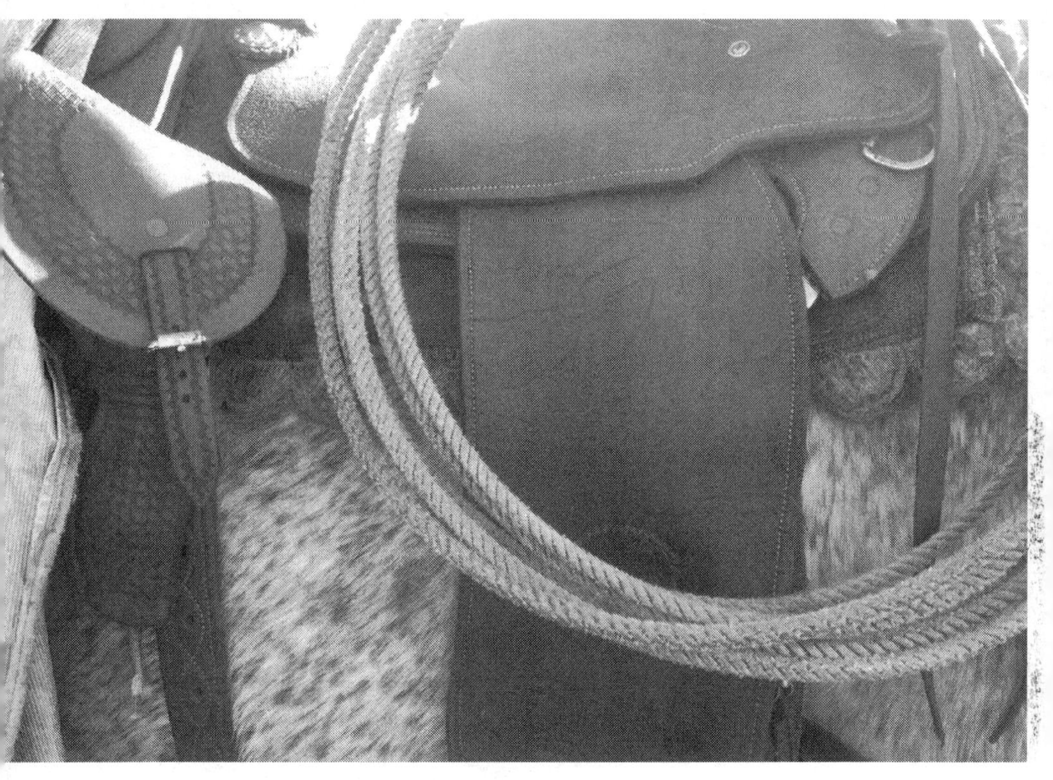

Tools of the trade, Lazy JP Ranch
Glades County, FL

Taking a midday water break at Lazy JP Ranch
Glades County, FL

BJ Johnson in one set of the pens at Lazy JP Ranch.
Glades County, FL

Fred Griffin and Troy Tomlinson (L-R) share a story at Buck Island Ranch near Lake Placid, Highlands County FL

Jacqueline Phares plays with one of the horses by braiding his mane during a break in the work at Lazy JP Ranch, Okeechobee, FL.

Brent Phares turning a cow back to the herd, Lazy JP Ranch. Glades County, FL

BJ Johnson and Brian Phares (L-R)
Lazy JP Ranch near Okeechobee,
Glades County, FL

A foggy morning at Buck Island Ranch near Lake Placid, FL in Highlands County

"Remnants of the Past"
Citrus trees like this one next to an old gate are
a commonly found nearby cow pens throughout Florida.

Seminole Tribe of Florida, Brighton Reservation
Glades County, FL

Alex Johns (foreground, right) and crew drive cattle through the trap and into the cow pens at sunrise on the Brighton Reservation.
Seminole Tribe of Florida, Glades County, FL

Matt Arrieta looking through some cows.
Lazy JP Ranch near Okeechobee, FL

BJ Johnson, Brent Phares, and Gus Leiva sharing a laugh as they bring cows into the pens. Lazy JP Ranch, Glades County, FL

Lazy JP Ranch cow pens, Glades County, FL

Celtic Cowhunter is a GenZ Publishing Book

GenZ™ is an innovative publishing platform for the new generation to have their work seen, recognized, published and read by millions. When an individual is chosen to be published on GenZ™, they can use that experience in their portfolios, for résumés, to share with friends, family, and fans. It is an accomplishment to be proud of for the rest of their lives.

We are on a mission to improve the world one word at a time. That is why we are the place for voices to be heard in a way not previously done in print and on digital media. It is a way to support young writers, our new voices.

It can be nearly impossible for young writers with promising talent to produce standout work that will be recognized, because of the state of the publishing and digital media industries. Having work recognized in a sea of so many writers is even tougher. That is why there is an underrepresentation of young and innovative voices in the publishing and print world. There are many unheard voices. GenZ is on a mission to change that.

GenZ™ provides a medium where these people can be positively recognized for their work through a professional product and supportive company.

Learn more about GenZ Publishing, how you can get involved, and all of our newest releases at GenZPublishing.org. Like us on Facebook at GenZ Publishing and follow us on Twitter @GenZPub.

Made in the USA
Charleston, SC
26 November 2016